T0230105

Lecture Notes in Computer Science

Lecture Notes in Computer Science

Edited by G. Goos and J. Hartmanis

337

Oliver Günther

Efficient Structures for Geometric Data Management

Springer-Verlag

Berlin Heidelberg New York London Paris Tokyo

Author

Oliver Günther
International Computer Science Institute
1947 Center Street, Suite 600
Berkeley, California 94704, USA

CR Subject Classification (1987): E.1, F.2.2, G.1.2, H.2.2, H.2.8, I.2.10, I.3.5, J.6

ISBN 3-540-50463-X Springer-Verlag Berlin Heidelberg New York
ISBN 0-387-50463-X Springer-Verlag New York Berlin Heidelberg

© Springer-Verlag Berlin Heidelberg 1988
Printed in Germany

Printing and binding: Druckhaus Beltz, Hemsbach/Bergstr.
2145/3140-543210

Meinen Eltern

Preface

This book is the revised and extended version of a Ph.D. dissertation submitted to the Department of Electrical Engineering and Computer Sciences, University of California at Berkeley. Many of the ideas presented in this book have their roots in discussions with Eugene Wong, my mentor and thesis advisor. I would like to thank Gene for being most supportive throughout the ups and downs of my years in graduate school. Our cooperation could not have been better.

Thanks to Mike Stonebraker for his advice and helpful criticism. Mike helped me get started at this university, and it was he who convinced me to stay in Berkeley beyond my Master's degree. Thanks also to the members of my thesis committee, Carlo Sequin and Dorit Hochbaum, for reading the various versions of my thesis and for providing me with several suggestions for improvement.

My years at Berkeley would not have been nearly as great without the loyal support of my best friends here and abroad: Grace Fan, Markus Flik, Michael Mast, Pietro Perona, Hans, Helga & Stefan Sprung, Magan Vikramsingh, Arnold Wassner and Andreas Weigend. I would also like to thank my colleagues in the INGRES group, at the International Computer Science Institute, and elsewhere: Jeff Bilmes, Peter Deussen, Joachim Diederich, Marc Fanty, Jerry Feldman, Eric Hanson, Yannis Ioannidis, Ron Kay, Werner Kiessling, Wolfgang Klas, Kurt Mehlhorn, Hanan Samet, Timos Sellis, Wolfgang Wahlster and many others who always had time for discussions and who gave me valuable suggestions, not only concerning my scientific work.

I would like to acknowledge the German National Scholarship Foundation, which first encouraged me to go abroad and supported me throughout the first three years at Berkeley with two scholarships. The National Science Foundation and the Army Research Office provided funding under grant numbers DMC-8300463 and ARO-DAAG 29-85-K-0223. The IBM corporation supported me during the final phase of my doctoral studies through their IBM Graduate Fellowship program, and the International Computer Science Institute provided me with the opportunity of spending eight more months at Berkeley as a postdoctoral fellow.

Finally, I would like to thank my parents Helmut und Helga Günther. Their support made this book possible; they were always there when I needed them. This book is dedicated to them.

And thanks to Carolyn, for sharing the best of times.

Berkeley, July 1988   Oliver Günther

Abstract

The efficient management of geometric data, such as points, curves, or polyhedra in arbitrary dimensions, is of great importance in many complex database applications like computer-aided design and manufacturing, robotics, or computer vision. To provide optimal support for geometric operators, it is crucial to choose efficient data representation schemes. In this monograph, we first give a taxonomy of operators and representation schemes for geometric data and conduct a critical survey of common representation schemes for two- and three-dimensional objects. Then we present several new schemes for the efficient support of set operators (union, intersection, difference) and search operators (point location, range search).

Polyhedral point sets are represented efficiently as *convex polyhedral chains*, i.e. algebraic sums of convex polyhedra (*cells*). Each cell in turn is represented as an intersection of halfspaces and encoded in a vector. The notion of vertices is abandoned completely. Then the computation of set operators can be decomposed into (a) a collection of vector operations, and (b) a garbage collection where vectors that represent empty cells are eliminated. All results of the garbage collection are cached in the vectors, which speeds up future computations. No special treatment of singular intersection cases is needed. This approach to set operations is significantly different from algorithms that have been proposed in the past.

To detect intersections of hyperplanes and convex polyhedra in arbitrary dimensions, we propose a *dual representation scheme* for polyhedra. In d dimensions, the time complexities of the dual algorithms are $O(2^d \log n)$ and $O((2d)^{d-1} \log^{d-1} n)$ for the hyperplane-polyhedron and the polyhedron-polyhedron intersection detection problems, respectively. In two dimensions, these time bounds are achieved with linear space and preprocessing. In three dimensions, the hyperplane-polyhedron intersection problem is also solved with linear space and preprocessing, which is an improvement over previously known results. Quadratic space and preprocessing, however, is required for the polyhedron-polyhedron intersection problem. For general d, the dual algorithms require $O(n^{2^d})$ space and preprocessing. These results are the first of their kind for dimensions greater than three. All of these results readily extend to unbounded polyhedra.

To support search operations, we introduce the *cell tree*, an index structure for geometric databases that is related to R-trees and BSP-trees. The data objects in the database are represented as convex polyhedral chains. The cell tree is a balanced tree structure whose leaves contain the cells and whose interior nodes correspond to a hierarchy of nested convex polyhedra. This index structure allows quick access to the cells (and thereby to the data objects), depending on their location in space. Furthermore, the cell tree is designed for paged secondary memory: each node corresponds to a disk page. This minimizes the number of page faults occuring during a search operation. Point locations and range searches can therefore be carried out very efficiently using the cell tree. The cell tree is a dynamic structure; insertions and deletions of cells cause only incremental changes. These update operations can be interleaved with searches and no periodic reorganization is required.

For the representation of arbitrary curved shapes, we introduce a hierarchical data structure termed *arc tree*. The arc tree is a balanced binary tree that represents a curve of length l such that any subtree whose root is on the k-th tree level is representing a subcurve of length $l/2^k$. Each tree level is associated with an approximation of the curve; lower levels correspond to approximations of higher resolution. Based on this hierarchy of detail, queries such as point inclusion or intersection detection and computation can be solved in a hierarchical manner. We present the results of a practical performance analysis for various kinds of set and search operators. Several related schemes are also discussed. Finally, we discuss various options to embed arc trees as complex objects in an extensible database management system like POSTGRES.

Table of Contents

Chapter 1

Introduction

Modern database systems are no longer limited to business applications. Non-standard applications such as robotics, computer vision, computer-aided design, or geographic data processing are becoming increasingly important, and geometric data play a crucial role in many of these new applications. For efficiency reasons it is essential that the special properties of geometric data be fully utilized in the database management system. It is important to view geometric objects (such as points, lines, polygons, polyhedra, or splines) as integral entities and not just as tuples of numbers that may be used to represent them.

Furthermore, the special operators that are defined on geometric data need to be supported. These operators are substantially different from the operators defined on numerical data. In particular, we distinguish between

- set operators: union, intersection, difference;

- search operators: point location (given a collection of geometric objects and a point, find all objects that contain the point), range search (given a collection of objects and a reference object, find all objects that intersect the reference object);

- similarity operators: translation, rotation, and scaling; and

- recognition operators: given a collection of geometric objects and a reference object, find all objects that resemble the reference object, according to some given metric.

With the possible exception of the similarity operators, all of these operators are harder to compute than most common numerical operators. To provide optimal support for an operator, it is important to choose an efficient scheme to represent the data. A representation scheme is the mapping of the original data objects into a set of objects that are convenient to store and that facilitate the computation of a particular class of operators.

Consider for example the various schemes to represent a polygon. By far, the most common way to represent a polygon is by a list of its vertices, given by their coordinates relative to some coordinate system. Clearly, the computation of similarity operators is fairly easy in this scheme; it just involves a simple numerical computation applied to all the coordinates. On the other hand, it is extremely difficult to compute recognition operators, as it is a non-trivial task to determine if two given vertex lists represent polygons that are similar, congruent, or even identical. In order to support recognition operators, it is necessary to normalize vertex lists, such that there is only one vertex list that represents a given polygon. Also, if two polygons are similar or congruent, their representations should have some components in common. Even normalized vertex lists, however, do not provide efficient support for set and search operators. For those operators, it is useful to represent polygons by means of a hierarchical scheme such as quadtrees, polyhedral chains, cell trees, or arc trees. These schemes will be discussed in detail in chapters 2, 3, 5, and 6, respectively.

In a numerical computing environment, it is often sufficient to maintain only one representation of the data. In geometric computing, on the other hand, it is often necessary to store multiple representations of the same data in order to facilitate the efficient computation of a great variety of geometric operators. Multiple representations cause a significant overhead to ensure availability and consistency of the data, and it is a subject of further research to see how extensible database management systems such as POSTGRES [Ston86a] can be used efficiently in such a complex data management environment.

The significance of representation schemes for efficient geometric data management was first recognized by Requicha, who gave an excellent taxonomy of geometric representation schemes in [Requ80]. This book continues in that direction: it starts with a survey of common operators and representation schemes for geometric data, then suggests some new schemes, and conducts several theoretical and practical analyses to determine which schemes are good for which operators. We also discuss how to embed these schemes in an extensible database management system like POSTGRES.

Chapter 2 considers some general properties of operators and representation schemes and gives a survey of common representation schemes for two- and three-dimensional geometric data. We propose several modifications to these schemes to eliminate some of their flaws. In particular, we discuss how to normalize representation schemes to be unique and to have invariants with respect to similarity operators. Then, a geometric object is represented by a unique tuple (g, z) where g is a set of similarity operators, and z is a description of the invariant parts of the object.

Furthermore, means for defining distance functions that measure the difference between two geometric objects are discussed. Distance functions are of great importance for the definition and support of recognition operators. As an example, Fourier descriptors [Pers77] to implement normalization and distance functions are considered.

Chapter 3 introduces polyhedral chains as a new representation scheme for general polyhedral point sets in arbitrary dimensions. Each polyhedral point set is represented as an algebraic sum of simple polyhedra (*cells*). In particular, we consider *convex* polyhedral chains, which contain only convex cells, and discuss an implementation where each cell is represented as an intersection of halfspaces and encoded in a ternary vector. The notion of vertices and adjacencies is abandoned completely. We show how this approach allows us to decompose the computation of set operators on polyhedral point sets into two independent steps. The first step consists of a collection of vector operations; the second step is a garbage collection where vectors that represent empty cells are eliminated. All results of the garbage collection are cached in the vectors, which speeds up future computations. No special treatment of singular intersection cases is needed. This approach to set operations is significantly different from algorithms that have been proposed in the past.

In order to carry out the garbage collection efficiently, an algorithm is needed to detect quickly whether two given convex cells intersect. Chapter 4 represents a digression into theoretical computational geometry: to detect intersections of hyperplanes and convex polyhedra in arbitrary dimensions, we propose a dual representation scheme for polyhedra. In d dimensions, the time complexities of the dual algorithms are $O(2^d \log n)$ and $O((2d)^{d-1} \log^{d-1} n)$ for the hyperplane-polyhedron and the polyhedron-polyhedron intersection detection problems, respectively. In two dimensions, these time bounds are achieved with linear space and preprocessing. In three dimensions, the hyperplane-polyhedron intersection problem is also solved with linear space and preprocessing, which is an improvement over previously known results. Quadratic space and preprocessing, however, is required for the polyhedron-polyhedron intersection problem. For general d, the dual algorithms require $O(n^{2^d})$ space and preprocessing. These results are the first of their kind for dimensions greater than three. All of these results readily extend to unbounded polyhedra.

Chapter 5 discusses geometric index structures that are used to support search operators such as point location or range search. We introduce the *cell tree*, an index structure for geometric databases that is related to R-trees [Gutt84] and BSP-trees [Fuch80, Fuch83]. The data objects in the database may be arbitrary point sets and are represented as convex polyhedral chains. The cell tree is a balanced tree structure whose leaves contain the cells and whose interior nodes correspond to a hierarchy of nested convex polyhedra. This index structure allows quick access to the cells (and thereby to the data objects), depending on their location in space. Furthermore, the cell tree is designed for paged secondary memory: each node corresponds to a disk page. This minimizes the number of page faults occuring during a search operation. Point locations and range searches can therefore be carried out very efficiently using the cell tree. The cell tree is a dynamic structure; insertions and deletions of cells cause only incremental changes. These update operations can be interleaved with searches and no periodic reorganization is required.

Chapter 6 introduces yet another hierarchical data structure. The *arc tree* represents a curve of length l by a balanced binary tree such that any subtree whose root is on the k-th tree level is representing a subcurve of length $l/2^k$. Each tree level is associated with an approximation of the curve; lower levels correspond to approximations of higher resolution. The arc tree can be viewed as just one instance of a large class of approximation schemes that implement some hierarchy of detail. Based on these data structures, queries such as point inclusion or intersection detection and computation can be solved in a hierarchical manner. Algorithms start out near the root of the tree and try to solve the queries at a very coarse resolution. If that is not possible, the resolution is increased where necessary. Chapter 6 contains the definition of the arc tree and a practical performance analysis for various kinds of set and search operators. We also discuss several related schemes and various options to embed arc trees as complex objects in an extensible database management system.

Chapter 7 contains our conclusions and directions for future work.

Chapter 2

Operators and Representation Schemes

for Geometric Data

2.1. Introduction

Many of the operators used in a geometric computation environment are substantially different from the operators defined on numerical data. They are often harder to compute, and it is not trivial to determine the smallest domain on which they are closed. The computation of search operators such as point location and range search, for example, usually requires complex hierarchical data structures such as the R-tree [Gutt84]. Set operators such as union or intersection are not even closed in the set of polyhedra (fig. 2.1).

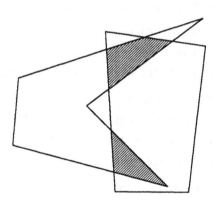

Figure 2.1: The intersection of two polyhedra is not always a polyhedron.

In short, to deal with geometric data effectively, it is important to support the computation of geometric operators by suitable representation schemes. Sections 2.2 and 2.3 consider some general properties of operators and representation schemes that are useful for classification and evaluation purposes. Sections 2.4 and 2.5 present an analysis of several representation schemes that are common in geometric applications. We distinguish between elementary and hierarchical representation schemes; hierarchical schemes represent an object by some combination of simpler objects of the same dimension. We propose several modifications to various schemes to eliminate some of their flaws. In particular, we discuss how to normalize representation schemes to be unique and to have invariants with respect to similarity operators. Then, a geometric object is represented by a unique tuple (g,z) where g is a sequence of similarity operators, and z is a description of the invariant parts of the object. Also, it is discussed how to define distance functions that measure the difference between two geometric objects. As an example, we discuss how to use Fourier descriptors [Pers77] to implement normalization and distance functions. Section 2.6 summarizes the results of this chapter in table format and gives a brief overview of the properties of the most common geometric representation schemes.

2.2. Properties of Operators

2.2.1. Operand and Result Spaces

An *operator* is a function $f: D_1^{k_1} \times D_2^{k_2} \times \ldots \times D_r^{k_r} \rightarrow R$. The D_i are the *operand spaces*, and R is the *result space* of the operator. Operators can be classified according to their result space, such as boolean operators, where $R = \{true, false\}$, or metric operators, where R is the set of real numbers.

Many common operators have only one operand space. They perform a mapping $D^k \rightarrow R$ and are called *homogeneous*. In this case, D is also called the *domain* of the operator. A homogeneous operator with $R = D$ is called *automorphic*. An automorphic operator is *closed* in D, or D is closed under the operator.

It is often desirable to have operators that are closed in some domain. In order to achieve this, one may embed an operator into another operator. An operator $f: D_1^{k_1} \times D_2^{k_2} \times \ldots \times D_r^{k_r} \rightarrow R$ is *embedded* in another operator $f_+: D_{1+}^{k_1} \times D_{2+}^{k_2} \times \ldots \times D_{r+}^{k_r} \rightarrow R_+$ if

(i) $D_i \subseteq D_{i+}$ ($i = 1 .. r$)

(ii) $R \subseteq R_+$

(iii) for all $(d_1 .. d_k) \in D_1^{k_1} \times D_2^{k_2} \times \ldots \times D_r^{k_r}$: $f(d_1 .. d_k) = f_+(d_1 .. d_k)$

2.2.2. Order

The sum $k_1+k_2+\ldots+k_r$ is the *order* of the operator. According to their order, operators are classified into unary, binary, ternary, or k-ary operators.

Many common operators are binary or can be reduced to a binary operator as follows. A set $\mathbf{F}=\{f_k:D^k\rightarrow D, k=1,2,3\ldots\}$ of automorphic operators is called a *family* of operators if for all $z\geq 1, i_1\ldots i_z\geq 1$, where $i_1+\ldots+i_z=k$, it is

$$f_k(p_1\ldots p_k)=f_z(f_{i_1}(p_1\ldots p_{i_1}),f_{i_2}(p_{i_1+1}\ldots p_{i_1+i_2})\ldots f_{i_z}(p_{i_1+\ldots+i_{z-1}+1}\ldots p_k))$$

Clearly, in a family (f_k) of operators, f_1 is the identical function. In particular, for $k\geq 2$ it is

$$f_k(p_1\ldots p_k)=f_2(f_2(\ldots(f_2(p_1,p_2),p_3)\ldots),p_k)$$

That is, each operator can be computed as a sequence of binary operators. The order of the operator is *reduced* to 2.

2.2.3. Invariants

Let G denote some group of unary automorphic operators on D, i.e. $G\subseteq\{g:D\rightarrow D\}$. The homogeneous operator $f:D^k\rightarrow R$ is *invariant* with respect to G if for all $g_i\in G$ $f(d_1,d_2,\ldots,d_k)=f(g_1d_1,g_2d_2,\ldots,g_kd_k)$. An important operator that is invariant with respect to similarity operators is the congruence test operator that tests two given geometric figures for congruence. Invariants may simplify the computation of such operators significantly; see section 2.3.4.

2.2.4. Commutativity and Associativity

A homogeneous operator f is *commutative* if for all $d_i\in D$ and all permutations Π it is $f(d_1,\ldots,d_k)=f(\Pi(d_1,\ldots,d_k))$.

A binary automorphic operator is *associative* if for all $d_i\in D$ $f(f(d_1,d_2),d_3)=f(d_1,f(d_2,d_3))$.

2.2.5. Examples: Numerical and Geometric Operators

The most common operators are the arithmetic operators $+$, $-$, $*$, and $/$. The addition operator $+$, for example, usually represents a family of automorphic, commutative, and associative operators on the domain of real numbers. It embeds the corresponding operators on the domains of rational or integer numbers. It is not invariant with respect to any non-trivial group of operators.

Another example is the division operator /. It usually represents a binary, automorphic, non-commutative, non-associative operator on the domain of real numbers. It embeds the corresponding operators on the domains of rational or integer numbers. Note, however, that the corresponding operator on integer numbers is not automorphic; the result space is, of course, the set of rational numbers.

In geometric applications, operators are often more complicated. That is, they are harder to compute, it is usually less trivial to determine the smallest result space in which they are closed, and it is harder to embed them into an automorphic operator. Consider, for example, the regularized intersection operator $\cap^*$, as defined by Tilove [Tilo80]. Given two point sets P and Q, this operator first obtains the simple intersection $P \cap Q$, and then computes the closure of its interior, yielding $P \cap^* Q$. This way, the dimension of the result is equal to the lowest dimension of any of the operands, and the resulting point set has no dangling edges or faces (fig. 2.2).

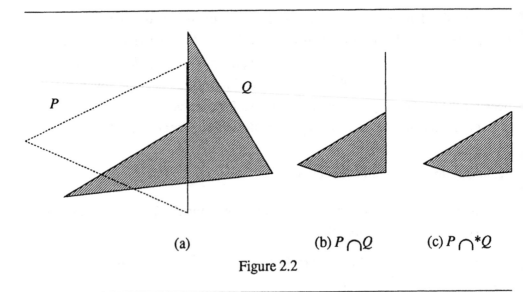

(a) (b) $P \cap Q$ (c) $P \cap^* Q$

Figure 2.2

The regularized intersection operator represents a family of commutative operators on the domain of d-dimensional polyhedra. Unfortunately, the operator is not closed in the set of polyhedra. It is only closed in the set of convex polyhedra or in the set of polyhedral chains, which are discussed in chapter 3. The remaining two regularized set operators, union ($\cup^*$) and difference ($-^*$), are both not even closed in the set of convex polyhedra. (They are closed, however, in the set of polyhedral chains.)

Other operators that are useful in geometric applications include the simple set operators, unary metric operators such as volume, unary automorphic operators such as the similarity operators (translation, rotation, and scaling), search operators such as point location and range search, and several binary boolean operators such as the tests for congruence or similarity, or the point inclusion test (given a point and a geometric object, is the point inside the object?). The volume, the congruence test, and the similarity test operator are all invariant with respect to the group of rigid body motions (i.e. translations and rotations). The similarity test operator is invariant with respect to the group of similarity operators.

2.3. Properties of Representation Schemes

Following Requicha [Requ80], a representation scheme is a relation $s: M \rightarrow R$. M, the modeling space, is a collection of objects to be represented. R, the representation space, is a collection of representations. For example, in the case of relational databases for geometric data, M contains multi-dimensional geometric objects, and R contains basic database objects such as tuples and relations.

2.3.1. Domain and Range

Requicha [Requ80] defines the *domain* D of s as the set of all representable objects, i.e. $D := \{m \in M : s(m) \neq \phi\}$. D should be as close to M as possible. The *range* V of s is the set of all valid representations in R. It is defined as $V := \{r \in R : s^{-1}(r) \neq \phi\}$. R-V should be minimized as invalid representations may cause various problems. They are often caused by redundancy in the representation.

2.3.2. Unambiguous and Unique Representations

A representation scheme s is *unambiguous* if $s^{-1}(v)$ is a single element set for each element v of V. It is *unique* if $s(d)$ is a single element set for each element d of D. Uniqueness is of crucial importance for recognition operators and in a database environment where one should be able to determine the identity of two objects immediately.

Non-unique representations schemes may be made unique by means of a *normalization function* $n: V \rightarrow V$, such that $n(v_1)=n(v_2)$ if and only if $s^{-1}(v_1)=s^{-1}(v_2)$. Then each object $d \in D$ may be represented by $n(s(d))$ rather than by $s(d)$, and V may be restricted to $n(V)$. The resulting representation scheme is clearly unique. Section 2.4.1 gives some examples on how to find a suitable normalization function to uniquely represent polygons and planar curves.

2.3.3. Irredundant and Concise Representations

Non−redundancy and *conciseness* are two properties of representation schemes that are harder to describe in a formal way. Informally spoken, a representation is non-redundant if there are no parts in the representation that are functionally dependent on other parts of the representation. A representation scheme is concise if it needs relatively little storage space for its representations; it contains few redundant data.

2.3.4. Invariants

Invariants are parts of a representation that do not change if certain operators are performed on the represented object. More formally, let G denote some group of unary automorphic operators on V, i.e. $G \subseteq \{g:V \rightarrow V\}$. The quotient V/G denotes the set of all equivalence classes in V under G. That is, each element in V/G is of the form $z = \{gv:g \in G\}$, $v \in V$. Now, $V = G \times V/G$, i.e. each element of V can be represented as $v = (g,z)$, $g \in G$, $z \in V/G$. Clearly, the z-part of this representation is invariant with respect to G, i.e. for all $\bar{g} \in G$ and all $(g,z) \in V$, it is $\bar{g}(g,z)=(\bar{g} \cdot g,z)$.

In a geometric environment it is highly desirable to have representation schemes that have invariants with respect to similarity operators. These invariants are useful to retrieve objects in the database that are congruent or similar to a given reference object.

An operator f that is invariant with respect to G can now be computed using only part of the representation:

$$f(v_1, v_2, \ldots, v_k)$$
$$= f((g_1, z_1), (g_2, z_2), \ldots, (g_k, z_k))$$
$$= f(g_1^{-1}(g_1, z_1), g_2^{-1}(g_2, z_2), \ldots, g_k^{-1}(g_k, z_k))$$
$$= f((\phi, z_1), (\phi, z_2), \ldots, (\phi, z_k)) \quad (\phi=\text{identity}).$$

The operator f can be computed using only the z-part of the representation, which may reduce the number of parameters considerably. An example for such an operator is the congruence test operator C that tests two given geometric figures for congruence. C is invariant with respect to the group of rigid body motions. Using the same notation as above, it is

$$C(v_1, v_2) = \begin{cases} true & \text{if } z_1 = z_2 \\ false & \text{otherwise} \end{cases}$$

The question is how to obtain a unique and concise representation of the invariants z of a given representation scheme. One possibility is to use a *normalization function* $n : V \rightarrow V$ such that $n(v_1) = n(v_2)$ if and only if v_1 and v_2 are equivalent under G. Clearly, $n(v_1) = n(v_2)$ is a concise representation of exactly those parts of v_1 and v_2 that are invariant under G, i.e. it is a representation of z. Section 2.4.1 gives some examples on how to find suitable normalization function for polygons and planar curves.

2.3.5. Distance Functions

In geometric applications it often happens that the given objects are slightly distorted. A geometric database system should therefore be able not only to retrieve objects that are identical to a given reference object, but also recognize objects that only resemble the reference object. Thus, one needs *distance functions* $d : V \times V \rightarrow E^1$ (E^1 denoting the set of real numbers) that measure the resemblance between two representations and that are fairly easy to compute. Of course, d should be a metric, i.e.

$$d(v_1, v_2) \geq 0, \quad d(v_1, v_2) = 0 \iff v_1 = v_2$$
$$d(v_1, v_2) = d(v_2, v_1)$$
$$d(v_1, v_3) \leq d(v_1, v_2) + d(v_2, v_3)$$

Furthermore, in most cases one would like the distance function to be invariant with respect to rigid body motions, i.e.

$$d(v_1, v_2) = d(gv_1, gv_2)$$

where g is a rigid body motion.

For an example, see section 2.4.1.2, where we show how to use Fourier descriptors [Pers77] to define distance functions on polygons and planar curves.

2.3.6. Continuity

Informally speaking, a representation scheme is *continuous* if it is robust with respect to slight changes and distortions; if an object changes slightly, then its representation should change only slightly as well. More formally, let p denote some appropriate distance function over the modeling space. Then a representation is continuous if $d(v_1, v_2)$ and $p(s^{-1}(v_1), s^{-1}(v_2))$ are roughly proportional for all $v_1, v_2 \in V$. Continuity alleviates the computation of recognition operators significantly, as similar objects always have similar representations.

A simple example for a continuous representation scheme are vertex lists to represent polygons. Local changes in the polygon shape cause only local changes in the corresponding vertex list. It is usually more difficult to find representations *with invariants* that are continuous because normalization functions are often very sensitive to changes of the input object. Normalization functions based on Fourier descriptors, however, do not have this disadvantage and lead to continuous representation schemes; see again section 2.4.1.2.

2.4. Elementary Representation Schemes

In this and the following section, we will describe and evaluate several common representation schemes for geometric data. An elementary representation scheme is a scheme in which the objects are *not* represented by some combination of simpler objects of the same dimension. Elementary representations include various boundary representation schemes, the sweep representation schemes, and the skeleton representation schemes.

2.4.1. Boundary Representation Schemes

2.4.1.1. Vertex Lists for General Polygons

By far, the most common way to represent a polygon is by a list of its vertices, given by their coordinates relative to some coordinate system. The vertex list is an unambiguous representation scheme that is easy to understand. It is able to represent any polygon, including polygons that are not simple (i.e. they may be self-intersecting or have holes). For some examples see figures 2.3a-c.

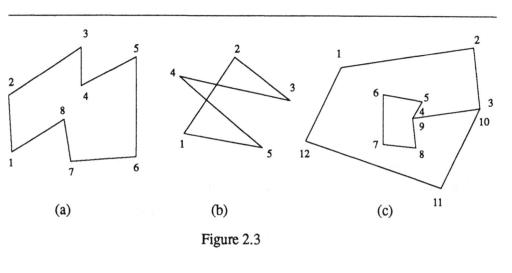

(a)　　　　　　　　　(b)　　　　　　　　　(c)

Figure 2.3

However, the vertex list representation has the following severe disadvantages. First, the representation is not unique. A circular shift of a vertex list produces another vertex list that describes the same polygon. In the case of a general n-gon without holes, there are n ways to construct a vertex list that represents the polygon. In the case of polygons with holes, the representation scheme maps each polygon into an even larger set of representations, as there are many ways to link a hole to its enclosing polygon (fig. 2.4a,b). The non-uniqueness of vertex lists makes the computation of recognition operators quite hard, as it is a non-trivial task to determine if two given vertex lists represent the same polygon.

Second, a vertex list does not contain any invariants with respect to the most common operators that are defined on polygons. Similarity operators will, in general, change each element of the representation, i.e. the representation does not

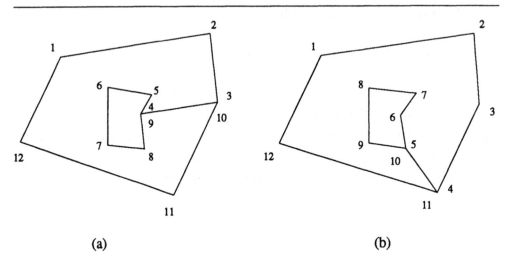

(a)   (b)

Figure 2.4

support any notion of congruence or similarity. There is no simple way to derive the fact that two polygons are congruent or similar from their vertex lists.

Third, storing a *list* (as opposed to a *set*) of vertices requires that the order of the list elements is maintained. This is inconvenient in a relational database environment, because relations are *sets* of tuples. In order to maintain an order among the tuples representing the vertices, one would have to introduce a special attribute *order—no*.

Finally, if vertex lists are used as a representation scheme for simple polygons only (i.e. no self-intersections or holes are allowed), there is an additional disadvantage. Not all vertex lists represent simple polygons, i.e. some vertex lists are invalid representations. There is no easy way to derive the fact that a polygon is simple from its vertex list.

There are several ways to modify vertex lists in a way that at least the most severe of these disadvantages are eliminated. In order to introduce uniqueness and invariants to the representation, one may normalize vertex lists by means of a *distinct vertex*. Then, each vertex list that represents a polygon may be required to have the distinct vertex as its first element. There are two features that characterize a given vertex: the lengths of the two adjacent edges, and the size of the corresponding interior angle. We base our definition of a distinct vertex on edge lengths because in practical applications, angles tend to be distributed much less equally than edge lengths (consider, for example, rectilinear polygons which constitute a large fraction of current applications).

We propose the following definition of a *distinct vertex*. Here, v denotes some vertex of a given polygon, α_v denotes the interior angle at vertex v, and w denotes v's neighbor vertex in counterclockwise direction. Let $EL(v)$ denote a sequence of edge lengths of the given polygon, starting with the length of edge (v,w), and proceeding counterclockwise. Analogously, let $AN(v)$ denote a sequence of angles of the given polygon, starting at angle α_v and proceeding counterclockwise. Finally, let $S(v)$ denote the concatenation of the sequences $EL(v)$ and $AN(v)$.

Given an n-gon P, its corresponding sequences $S(v_1), S(v_2), \ldots, S(v_n)$ can be sorted by increasing first element. In case of a tie, the corresponding sequences are sorted by increasing second element, and so on. The result is a sorted array of sequences, and the distinct vertex is defined as the vertex $\bar{v}$ where $S(\bar{v})$ is the first sequence in that sorted array. If there are several vertices $v_1, v_2 .. v_k$ that tie for the distinct vertex, then any of those vertices may be declared distinct.

Note that the distinct vertex of a polygon is defined in a way that is invariant with respect to similarity operators. In particular, we propose to represent a polygon P, given by its vertex list in conventional form,

$$\{(x_1,y_1), (x_2,y_2), \ldots, (x_n,y_n)\}$$

by the *factorized vertex list*,

$$\{\alpha, x_\gamma, y_\gamma, s, (\overline{x_1},\overline{y_1}), (\overline{x_2},\overline{y_2}), \ldots, (\overline{x_{n-2}},\overline{y_{n-2}})\}$$

such that

$$P = t_\gamma \cdot ro_\alpha \cdot sc_s \cdot \bar{P}$$

where x_γ and y_γ are the coordinates of the distinct vertex, t_γ is the translation defined by the vector (x_γ, y_γ), ro_α is the rotation about the origin by angle α, sc_s is the scaling about the origin with ratio s, and $\bar{P}$ is the polygon represented by the vertex list (in conventional form)

$$\{(0,0), (1,0), (\overline{x_1},\overline{y_1}), (\overline{x_2},\overline{y_2}), \ldots, (\overline{x_{n-2}},\overline{y_{n-2}})\}$$

This representation is unique with respect to all polygons without holes, and it has invariant components with respect to all similarity operators. In particular, two polygons are similar if and only if their representations only differ in their corresponding values for $\alpha, x_\gamma, y_\gamma$ and s. Two polygons are congruent if they are similar and if their corresponding values for s are identical.

Based on this representation, a polygon may be represented in a relational database in two relations *polygons* and *coordinates* which may be defined as follows.

> *polygons* (*pol–id* = int, α = real, x_γ = real, y_γ = real, s = real,
>
> *vlist* = *coordinates using pol–id*)
>
> *coordinates* (*pol–id* = int, x = real, y = real, *order–no* = int)

Here, *vlist* is an attribute of data type *relation*, as defined by Wong [Wong85]. Each value of this domain consists of the set of tuples of *coordinates* sharing the same *pol–id* value. These tuples contain the coordinates $\overline{x_1}, \overline{y_1}, \overline{x_2}, \overline{y_2} \ldots \overline{x_{n-2}}, \overline{y_{n-2}}$. Note that *coordinates* has to have an attribute *order–no* to keep the vertex list sorted.

This representation still has some of the disadvantages we mentioned above. First, it does not provide a unique way to represent polygons with holes. For this case, a hierarchical representation scheme seems to be a better solution. Second, each representation is still a list and not a set of vertices. Third, for the case of simple polygons, it still produces invalid representations. The integrity constraint that it represents a simple polygon can not be easily enforced. However, there exist standard algorithms to test a given vertex list in time $O(n \log n)$ if it represents a simple polygon; see for example [Prep85], pp. 271-279.

The described scheme of the factorized vertex list is unique for polygons without holes and it is unambiguous, but unfortunately it is not continuous. Slight distortions of a given polygon might change its representation fundamentally. Also, it is an ad hoc scheme, which is not theoretically sound. A better approach to normalization are Fourier descriptors, which will be discussed in the following section.

2.4.1.2. Fourier Descriptors for Planar Curves

Another way to represent polygons is based on the use of the Fourier transformation. This representation scheme has been introduced by Zahn and Roskies [Zahn72] and refined later by Persoon and Fu [Pers77]. It is a much more general scheme as it can be used to represent not only polygons, but general planar curves as well.

The idea is to view a given curve as a path in the complex plane and to parametrize it with respect to its arc length. The x- and y-coordinates of each curve point become complex numbers $x+iy$, and the curve becomes a function $c : [0,1] \rightarrow C$, where C denotes the set of complex numbers. Then one computes the *Fourier descriptors (FDs)* of the function $c(t)$ ($t \in [0,1]$); the Fourier descriptors γ_n ($n=0,\pm1,\pm2 \dots$) are complex numbers with

$$\gamma_n = \frac{1}{2\pi} \int_{-\pi}^{\pi} c(t) \cdot e^{-int} \, dt$$

Then it is

$$c(t) = \sum_{n=-\infty}^{+\infty} \gamma_n \cdot e^{int}$$

Now, a curve is represented by a vector of complex numbers; in practice, only a finite number of FDs ($\gamma_{-N} \dots \gamma_N$) may be stored, which corresponds to an approximation of the original curve. Note that for $n \neq 0$ the FDs γ_n are invariant with respect to translations of the corresponding curve.

Given a function $c(t)$, the FDs corresponding to this function are uniquely defined. Nevertheless, the representation scheme is not unique at this point. The function $c(t)$ describing the curve varies with the choice of the starting point $c(0)$; there are infinitely many functions $c(t)$ describing the same curve. Also, the scheme does not have any explicit invariances with respect to rotations and scalings. However, a simple normalization function can eliminate the dependency of FDs on starting point, orientation, and size. The resulting normalized representation scheme is unique and has invariances with respect to similarity operators, such that it allows an easy matching of a given curve against a database of curves, regardless of its original starting point, orientation, and size.

The operators in the representation space that affect the starting point, orientation, and size of the original curve follow directly from properties of the Fourier transformation. To change the size of the curve simply corresponds to a multiplication of the FDs by a real constant. A rotation of the curve corresponds to a multiplication of each FD by $e^{i\Theta}$, where Θ is the angle of rotation ($\Theta \in [0, 2\pi]$). To move the starting point by a phase angle Φ corresponds to a multiplication of the n-th FD γ_n by $e^{in\Phi}$ ($\Phi \in [0, 2\pi]$).

Given the FDs of an arbitrary curve, the normalization function should yield a standard size, orientation, and starting point. A standard size is easily defined by requiring the FD γ_1 to have unity magnitude. The normalization of orientation and starting point affects only the phases of the FDs. Since there are two allowable operations, the definition of standard orientation and starting point must involve the phases of at least two FDs. One obvious choice is to require the phases of both γ_1 and γ_2 to be zero. This normalization scheme works fine, although the practical implementation requires paying attention to a few details and some special cases, which are beyond the scope of this presentation.

In the resulting representation scheme, a curve c is represented by the FDs of the normalized version $\bar{c}$ of c, a rotation angle α, and a scaling factor s, such that

$$c = t_{\gamma_0} \cdot ro_\alpha \cdot sc_s \cdot \bar{c}$$

Here, t_{γ_0} denotes the translation by $\text{Re}(\gamma_0)$ in x-direction and $\text{Im}(\gamma_0)$ in y-direction. Remember that all components of the representation except γ_0 are invariant with respect to translations.

This normalized representation scheme has several advantages. It is unique and it has invariances with respect to all similarity operators. If the input curve is a polygon, then the integrals above are discrete and the representation is very easy to compute. Furthermore, the representation scheme is continuous, i.e. it is robust with respect to slight changes and distortions of a given curve. In particular, the normalization function is very robust; similar curves are mapped into curves with a similar orientation, size, and starting point. For some examples, see figure 2.5. These results have been obtained from our implementation of FDs on a VAX 8800; each normalization took between 8 ms and 12 ms CPU time.

Finally, any norm defined on complex vectors may be used to define the distance d between two representations. Using the Euclidean metric, for example, the distance between two given representations $r = (\gamma_{-N} \dots \gamma_N)$ and $\bar{r} = (\overline{\gamma_{-N}} \dots \overline{\gamma_N})$ becomes

$$d(r,\bar{r}) = \left[\sum_{n=-N}^{N} |\gamma_n - \overline{\gamma_n}|^2 \right]^{1/2}$$

This metric has been used succesfully by Persoon and Fu [Pers77] to recognize handwritten characters.

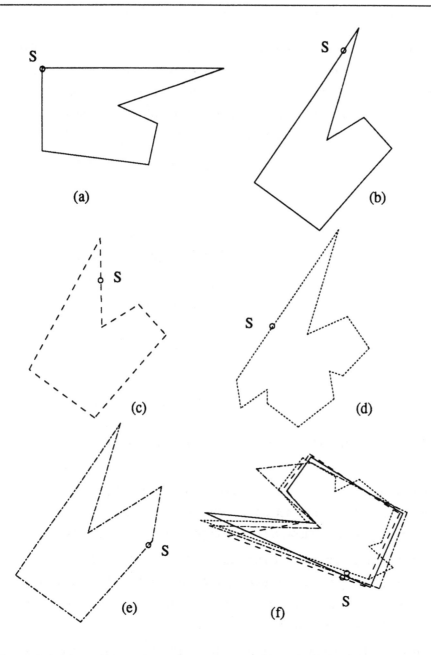

Figure 2.5: The polygons (a) - (e) are mapped onto the polygons in (f). Note that the polygons (a) and (b) are congruent. S denotes the starting point.

2.4.1.3. B-Rep and Wireframe for Three-Dimensional Objects

This and the following section are based on [Besl85], an overview of three-dimensional object recognition. Surface boundary representations, or *B-Reps*, define a solid object by a list of the three-dimensional surfaces that bound that object. For example, a tetrahedron can be described by a set of four triangles in three-dimensional space. Another more complex example is given in figure 2.6.

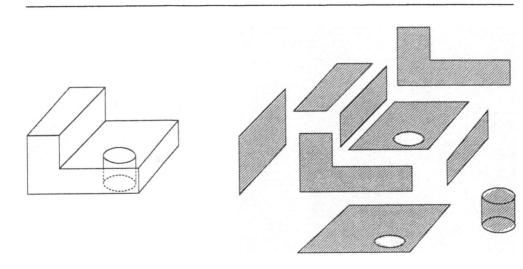

Figure 2.6: Surface boundary representation of a solid object (from [Requ83]).

Arbitrary surfaces can be approximated to any desired degree of accuracy by utilizing more faces. Even more accuracy is obtained using boundary representations that are based on quadric surfaces, higher order polynomials and splines.

All of these representation schemes are unambiguous for all polyhedra with planar faces, and they approximate curved objects arbitrarily well. Depending on the surface representation, they may have invariants with respect to translation operators, where the slopes of the surfaces remain the same.

However, surface boundary representations are not unique and they contain invalid representations. They do not provide good support for search, set, or recognition operators. Surface boundary representations also may contain redundancies if, for example, edges are defined in both adjacent surfaces. This flaw has been corrected in some modern display systems such as UNIGRAFIX [Sequ83, Sequ85] where the actual geometry is stored only in the coordinates of the vertices. Higher-dimensional objects such as edges of faces are defined by means of pointers: an edge is represented by two pointers to its endpoints, a face by pointers to the edges of its boundary, and so on. In this case, the B-Rep scheme corresponds to a hierarchy of three abstraction levels (faces, edges, and vertices), which leads to several possibilities to utilize B-Reps in a geometric database environment; see [Meie86] or [Kemp87a] for details.

Another boundary representation scheme is the wireframe scheme that defines a solid object by a list of its edges in space. This representation scheme is only suitable to represent polyhedra with planar faces. Of course, the slopes of the edges are invariant with respect to translations, and the lengths are invariant with respect to all rigid body motions. The wireframe representation scheme has the same disadvantages as the surface boundary representation scheme; moreover, it is ambiguous (fig. 2.7).

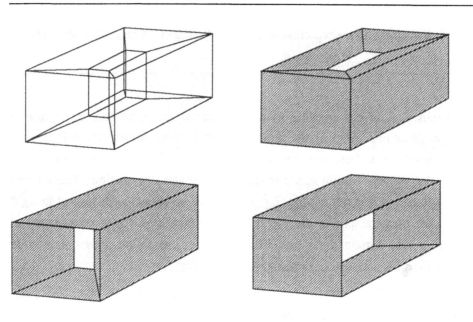

Figure 2.7: Wireframe ambiguity (from [Requ82]).

2.4.2. Sweep Representation Schemes

In sweep representations of three-dimensional objects, the object is represented by a space curve which acts as the spine or axis of the object, a two-dimensional cross-sectional figure, and a sweeping rule which defines how the cross-section is swept and possibly modified along the space curve. For an example see figure 2.8. Sweep representations can also be applied to two-dimensional objects.

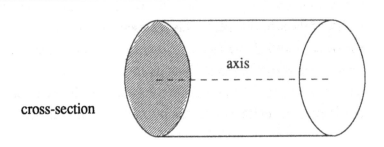

Figure 2.8: Sweeping rule: keep cross-section constant and orthogonal to the axis.

Obviously, it is not possible to represent arbitrary point sets by means of sweep representations. Also, if the representation scheme is used for polygons or simple point sets, then there exist invalid representations because sweep representations may also represent point sets that are curved or self-intersecting. The scheme is unambiguous, but it is not unique (fig. 2.9). It has invariants with respect to rigid body motions; only the axis of the object has to be modified, the cross-section and the sweeping rule remain the same. The sweep representation does not provide efficient support for set, search, or recognition operators.

2.4.3. Skeleton Representation Schemes

Skeleton schemes represent a geometric object by means of a graph. The edges of the graph correspond to *axes* or to a *skeleton* of the object and are obtained via a skeletonizing algorithm. One way to define a skeleton is by means of the medial axis tranformation (MAT), as proposed by Blum [Blum67]. The MAT of an object m with boundary b is defined as follows. For each point p in m, we find its closest

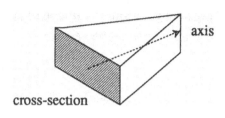
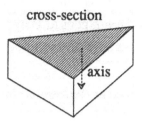

(a) sweeping rule: scale down the cross-section linearly from its original size to zero.

(b) sweeping rule: keep the cross-section constant.

Figure 2.9: Non-uniqueness of sweep representations.

neighbor in b. If p has more than one such neighbor, then it belongs to the *medial axis* (skeleton) of m. Some two-dimensional examples (using the Euclidean distance) are given in figure 2.10.

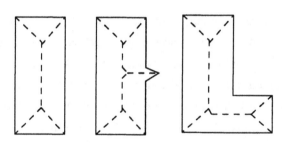

Figure 2.10: The medial axis transformation of three regions (from [Gonz87]).

Although the MAT yields an intuitively pleasing skeleton, a direct implementation of the above definition is clearly impossible as it involves calculating the distance from every interior point to every point of the object boundary. Some more practical skeletonizing algorithms have been developed by Dyer and Rosenfeld [Dyer79], Salari and Siy [Sala84], and Zhang and Suen [Zhan84].

Obviously, skeleton schemes are not always applicable, and they are neither unique nor unambiguous. They are useful for giving a rough, short description of an object, but they are certainly not a general-purpose representation scheme.

2.5. Hierarchical Representation Schemes

In a hierarchical representation scheme, the objects are represented by some combination of simpler objects of the same dimension. The most common hierarchical representation schemes are occupancy schemes and constructive solid geometry (CSG). In chapter 3 we propose a new hierarchical representation scheme, termed polyhedral chains.

2.5.1. Occupancy Representation Schemes

Occupancy representations define an object by *non−overlapping* regions of space occupied by a particular object. They uniquely define the geometric extension of an object. Usually, the regions are organized in some kind of hierarchical data structure in order to facilitate the computation of set and search operators.

A very common occupancy representation scheme for two-dimensional data is the quadtree [Fink74, Same84], and in particular the region quadtree as a representation scheme for bounded two-dimensional point sets. Suppose, the point set is given as a two-dimensional array of 1's and 0's. The region quadtree is based on the successive subdivision of this image array into four equal-sized quadrants. If the array does not consist entirely of 1's or entirely of 0's, it is then subdivided into quadrants, subquadrants, etc. until blocks are obtained (possibly single pixels) that consist entirely of 1's or entirely of 0's; that is, each block is entirely contained in the point set or entirely disjoint from it.

For example, consider the polygon in figure 2.11a, which is represented by the 2^3 by 2^3 binary array in figure 2.11b. The 1's correspond to pixels inside the point set and the 0's correspond to pixels outside the point set. The resulting blocks for the array of figure 2.11b are shown in figure 2.11c. The subdivision process is represented by a 4-ary tree; the root node corresponds to the whole array, and each son of a node represents a quadrant of the (sub)array represented by that node (fig. 2.11d).

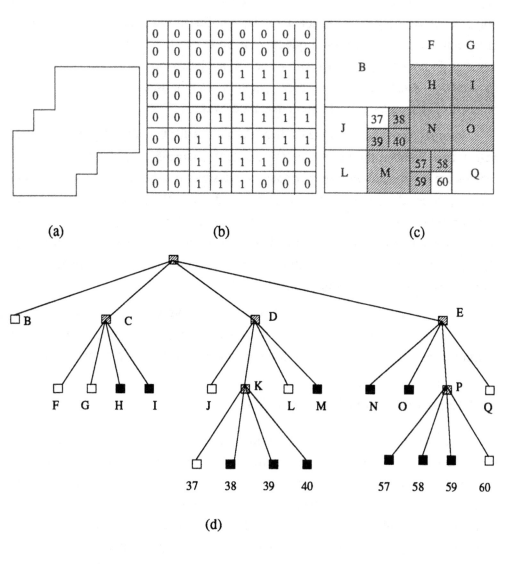

0	0	0	0	0	0	0	0
0	0	0	0	0	0	0	0
0	0	0	0	1	1	1	1
0	0	0	0	1	1	1	1
0	0	0	1	1	1	1	1
0	0	1	1	1	1	1	1
0	0	1	1	1	1	0	0
0	0	1	1	1	0	0	0

(a)   (b)   (c)

(d)

Figure 2.11: A quadtree (from [Same84]).

Other common occupancy representation schemes include the octtree, a three-dimensional version of the quadtree, or the general voxel representation, where an object is represented by a list of disjoint identical geometric primitives.

The most severe drawbacks of these occupancy schemes are that they require a lot of storage space and that they are ambiguous. Usually, they only represent an approximation of the actual object, based on the primitives provided. For example, a polygon whose edges are diagonal to the rectilinear quadtree grid can only be represented *approximately* by a quadtree of finite depth. Furthermore, occupancy schemes do not have invariants with respect to similarity operators. On the contrary, they are very sensitive to any of these operators; a slight translation or rotation of an object may change its representation in a major way.

In order to overcome some of those difficulties for the case of polygonal data, Samet and Webber proposed the PM quadtree [Same85]. In the PM quadtree, regions are subdivided until they contain only a small number of polygon edges and vertices; these edges and vertices are then stored explicitly in the leaves of the tree. PM quadtrees store polygonal maps (i.e. collections of polygons, possibly containing holes) without any loss of information. They are not overly sensitive to the positioning of the map. A generalization to three dimensions has been discussed by Navazo *et al.* [Ayal85, Nava86, Brun87].

For the reasons mentioned above, occupancy representation schemes are usually not used as a main representation scheme; they may, however, be used as an additional representation to support the computation of set and search operators.

2.5.2. Constructive Solid Geometry (CSG)

The CSG representation of a three-dimensional object is specified in terms of a set of three-dimensional volumetric primitives (blocks, cylinders, cones, and spheres are typical examples of bounded primitives), and a set of geometric operators. The object is represented by a binary tree (the CSG-tree) whose interior nodes correspond to similarity operators or regularized set operators. The leaves of the CSG-tree correspond to primitives or to numerical arguments to the similarity operators. For an example see figure 2.12. The primitives are represented by means of a non-hierarchical scheme as described in section 2.4. Note that the depth of the CSG-tree may vary, depending on the complexity of the object to be represented. For an analysis how the CSG representation scheme may be used in geometric databases, see [Meie86] or [Kemp87a].

CSG-trees provide an unambiguous scheme to represent any three-dimensional object. Set and similarity operators can be carried out in a trivial manner by creating a new root node containing the given operator. In the case of a set operators, the CSG-trees of the two operands are attached to the new root. For similarity operators,

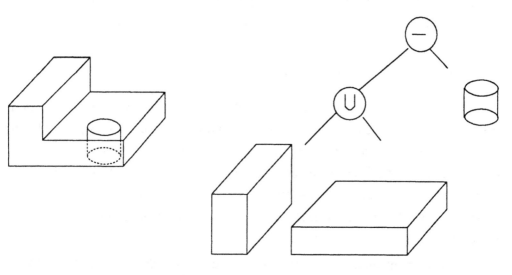

Figure 2.12: CSG representation of a solid object (from [Requ83]).

one descendant of the new root is the old CSG-tree, the other one contains the numerical arguments required.

The drawbacks of CSG are as follows. CSG is not a unique representation scheme. Search operators are very hard to compute: in order to determine if a given point is inside or outside the object, for example, one has to solve the point inclusion problem for each primitive in the corresponding CSG-tree. Then the CSG-tree has to be traversed to combine the results. A further disadvantage of the CSG representation is that it is hard to render the boundary of an object from its CSG-tree. Also, it is difficult to determine if a given CSG-tree represents a non-empty point set [Tilo84].

Of course, it is possible to generalize CSG to two or more than three dimensions. The properties of the representation scheme remain the same.

Together with the B-Rep scheme (see section 2.4.1.3), the CSG representation scheme is the most important representation scheme for rigid solids in current CAD/CAM systems. It is possible to transform a CSG representation to a B-Rep automatically. In many geometric modeling systems, the input is performed via CSG, which is much more user-friendly than B-Rep. For further computations, the

CSG representation is then transformed internally into B-Rep. For each object in the database, both representations are stored and kept mutually consistent.

2.5.3. Halfspaces for Convex Polyhedra

One variation of the CSG representation scheme deserves some more attention because it evades some of the disadvantages mentioned above. Convex polyhedra in Euclidean space E^d can be represented as the intersection of some finite number of closed halfspaces in E^d. On the other hand, each halfspace HS can be represented by means of a vector $a \in E^d-\{0\}$ and a real number c, such that $HS(a,c) = \{x \in E^d: x \cdot a \geq c\}$. Here, $x \cdot y$ denotes the inner product of vector x and vector y.

This representation scheme is unambiguous, and it does not contain invalid representations. The order of the halfspaces is insignificant, which is convenient if the representation scheme is used in a relational database system where the maintenance of an order requires additional space and overhead.

The representation scheme has invariants with respect to translations: the a-vectors remain unchanged. This property somewhat facilitates the computation of translation operators. The representation scheme does not have any invariants or provide any other support for other similarity operators. In particular, there is no simple way to derive the fact that two convex polygons are congruent or similar from their representations.

Given two convex polyhedra P and Q, their regularized intersection $P \cap^* Q$ may be represented simply by the union of the sets of halfspaces representing P and Q. The union and difference operators are not closed in the set of convex polyhedra and can therefore not be computed within this representation scheme.

Note that this scheme is not necessarily unique because any given representation may contain any number of *redundant* halfspaces, i.e. halfspaces $HS(a,c)$ whose bounding hyperplane $H(a,c) = \{x \in E^d: x \cdot a = c\}$ does not embed a $(d-1)$-dimensional face of the polyhedron. To make the representation scheme unique, redundant hyperplanes must not be allowed; each representation must only contain a *minimum* set of halfspaces. The computation of $P \cap^* Q$ then has to be extended by a postprocessing step where all redundant halfspaces are deleted from the representation of $P \cap^* Q$.

Using this representation schemes for convex polyhedra, one could then represent general polyhedra in Euclidean space E^d as a union of convex components. This proposal is discussed in much detail in chapter 3, where we introduce the concepts of polyhedral chains and h-vectors.

2.6. Summary - Evaluation of Representation Schemes

In the following table, M, D, R, and V denote the modeling space, the domain, the representation space, and the range of a representation scheme. T stands for the translation operator, M stands for the group of rigid body motions (i.e. translations and rotations), S stands for the group of similarities (i.e. rigid body motions and scalings), and R denotes recognition operators. Properties of simple set operators ($\cup$, $\cap$, and $-$) also hold for the corresponding regularized set operators ($\cup^*$, $\cap^*$, and $-^*$).

Besides the representation schemes discussed in this chapter, the table also includes information about various kinds of polyhedral chains and about a dual representation scheme. These representation schemes will be discussed in detail in chapters 3 and 4, respectively.

Representation Sch.	M	D=M	R	V=R	unamb.	unique	Invariants	V closed w.r.t.	Supported Op's
Set of halfspaces	convex polyhedra	y	set of halfspaces	y	y	n	T	S,∩	T,∩
Min. set of halfspaces	convex polyhedra	y	set of halfspaces	y	y	y	T	S,∩	T,∩
Dual space	convex polyhedra	y	two functions $E^{d-1} \to E^1$	n	y	y	T	S,∩	intersection detection
Vertex list	simple polygons	y	vertex list	n	y	n	-	S	S
Factorized vertex list	simple polygons	y	fact. vertex list	n	y	y	S	S	S,R
Skeleton schemes	simple polygons	y	set of axes	n	n	n	T	S	R
Vertex list	general polygons	y	vertex list	y	y	n	-	S	S
Factorized vertex list	general polygons	y	fact. vertex list	y	y	n	S	S	S
Normal'd Fourier desc.	general polygons	y	seq. complex nos.	n	y	n	S	S	S,R
Sweep representation	general polygons	n	axis, cross section & sweeping rule	n	y	n	M	S	M
Occupancy schemes	general polygons	y	quadtree or set of primitives	y†	n	y	-	S,∪,∩,-	∪,∩,-
CSG	general polygons	y	CSG-tree	y†	y	n	S	S,∪,∩,-	S,∪,∩,-
Polyhedral chains + factorized vertex list	general polygons	y	2-D polyhedral chain	y	y	n	S	S,∪,∩,-	S,∪
Convex polyhedral chains + h-vector	general polygons	y	2-D polyhedral chain	y	y	n	-	S,∪,∩,-	∪,∩,-
B-Rep	3-D polyhedra	y	set of polygons	n	y	n	T	S	T
Wireframe	3-D polyhedra	y	set of edges	n	n	n	T	S	T
Sweep representation	3-D polyhedra	n	axis, cross section & sweeping rule	n	y	n	M	S	M
Skeleton schemes	3-D polyhedra	y	set of axes	n	n	n	T	S	R
Occupancy schemes	3-D polyhedra	y	octree or set of primitives	y†	y	y	-	S,∪,∩,-	∪,∩,-
CSG	d-D polyh. (d≥3)	y	CSG-tree	y†	y	n	S	S,∪,∩,-	S,∪,∩,-
Polyhedral chains	d-D polyh. (d≥3)	y	polyhedral chain	y	y	n	††	S,∪,∩,-	∪,∩††
Convex polyhedral chains + h-vector	d-D polyh. (d≥3)	y	polyhedral chain	y	y	n	-	S,∪,∩,-	∪,∩,-

† if the primitives are polygonal/polyhedral point sets as well   †† depending on the representation scheme for the cells: S

Chapter 3

Polyhedral Chains

3.1. Introduction

In this chapter, we consider the representation of a particularly important class of geometric objects, viz., general polyhedra in arbitrary dimensions. The restriction to polyhedra, rather than general point sets, is justified by the fact that those are commonly used to approximate general shapes in practice [Faux79].

In most current applications the polyhedra to be represented are simple, i.e. self-intersections or holes are not allowed. Non-simple polyhedra, however, become more and more important in areas like computer-aided design or geographic data processing. Several examples for the applications of self-intersecting polygons in the area of IC mask description are given in [Newe80]. Geographic applications very often need polygons with holes (for example, to represent areas whose altitude is within a given range). Some applications may require polygons that are folded and keep track of the resulting multiple layers. Also, there are numerous applications for higher-dimensional or unbounded polyhedra, such as linear programming [Dant63] or logic databases where geometric objects are used to represent predicates [Ston86b].

A representation scheme for polyhedra should therefore include polyhedra in higher dimensions as well as polyhedra that are unbounded or non-simple. Furthermore, it has to support some of the most common operators performed on geometric data, such as set and search operators. Finally, the representation scheme should be closed under set operators.

This chapter, which is an extended version of [Gunt87a], presents the idea of polyhedral chains as a representation scheme for general polyhedra in arbitrary dimensions that meets these challenges. A general polyhedron may be self-intersecting or unbounded, it may have holes, and it may consist of several disjoint pieces. However, the polyhedra considered here are assumed to be regular [Tilo80], i.e. closed and without degenerate parts, such as a dangling edge or face (one that bounds nothing). Furthermore, all set operators in this chapter are assumed to be regularized, unless stated otherwise.

General polyhedra are represented as polyhedral chains, i.e. algebraic sums of simple polyhedra (*cells*). In sections 3.2 and 3.3, we give a definition of polyhedral chains and discuss their properties. Sections 3.4 and 3.5 describe in detail a representation scheme that is based on *convex* polyhedral chains, which have only convex cells. Each cell in turn is represented as the intersection of halfspaces and encoded in a vector. The notion of vertices is abandoned completely as it is not needed for the set and search operators we intend to support.

In section 3.6, it is shown how this approach allows us to decompose the computation of set operators on polyhedra into two steps. The first step consists of a collection of vector operations; the second step is a garbage collection where vectors that represent empty cells are eliminated. No special treatment of singular intersection cases such as dangling edges or faces is needed. This approach to set operations is significantly different from algorithms that have been proposed in the past [Fran82, Mant82, Mant83, Tilo84b, Requ85, Carl87]. Most of those approaches are based on a space partitioning to localize the set operations and on the subsequent use of vertices, edges, and adjacencies. They require special treatment for singular intersection cases and are difficult to generalize to higher dimensions. A first algorithm for the treatment of higher-dimensional polyhedra has appeared recently [Putn86]. Like some of the algorithms mentioned above, it uses a complicated boundary classification scheme, which involves special treatment of singular intersection cases.

For the computation of search operators using convex polyhedral chains, see chapter 5.

3.2. Definition

In order to meet the demands mentioned above, we extend the notion of polyhedron in the following way. A *polyhedral chain* in d-dimensional Euclidean space $\mathbf{E}^d$, as defined by Whitney [Whit57], is an expression of the form

$$\sum_{i=1}^{m} \alpha_i p_i$$

where α_i are integers and p_i are simple d-dimensional polyhedra in $\mathbf{E}^d$, called *cells*. The cells are closed, but not necessarily bounded. The algebraic convention is as follows:

$$\alpha p_i + \beta p_i = (\alpha + \beta) p_i$$

$$p_i + p_j = p_i \cup p_j \quad \Longleftrightarrow \quad p_i \cap p_j = \phi$$

$$0 \cdot p_i = \phi$$

Two polyhedral chains are *equivalent* if they can be transformed into each other using these conventions.

The semantics assigned to a polyhedral chain are as follows. The polyhedral chain can be viewed as a function that maps each point $t \in E^d$ into an integer number that indicates the number of cells present at this point. More formally, the function f_x corresponding to a chain $x = \sum\limits_{i=1}^{m} \alpha_i p_i$ may be defined as

$$f_x(t) = \sum_{t \in p_i} \alpha_i \quad , t \in E^d$$

From the algebraic conventions for polyhedral chains it follows that two chains are equivalent if and only if they correspond to the same function $f_x(t)$.

Polyhedral chains are a simple and powerful tool to describe various kinds of polyhedra. They may be used to describe any polyhedral point set in E^d (fig. 3.1a), as well as self-intersecting polyhedra of any shape (fig. 3.1b, 3.1c).

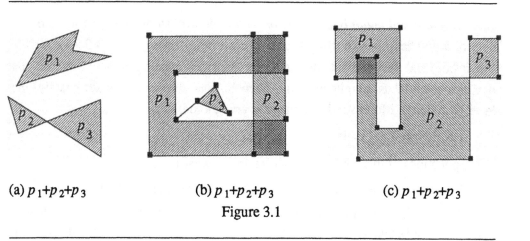

(a) $p_1 + p_2 + p_3$ (b) $p_1 + p_2 + p_3$ (c) $p_1 + p_2 + p_3$

Figure 3.1

In many applications, one distinguishes between the inside and the outside of a polyhedron. Given a polyhedral chain x_P, there are several conventions in common use to determine whether a given point $t \in E^d$ is to be considered inside or outside the corresponding polyhedral point set $P \subseteq E^d$. These include the parity, the oriented multiply-covered, and the nonzero winding number convention [Newe80].

The *parity convention* determines the state of a point by the parity of the number of intersections between faces of the polyhedron P and a straight line drawn from the point to infinity in any direction (fig. 3.2). Therefore,

$$t \in P \iff f_{x_P}(t) \text{ is odd.}$$

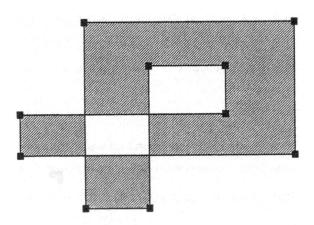

Figure 3.2: Parity convention (from [Newe80]).

The *oriented multiply-covered convention* defines an orientation for the boundary of a polyhedron such that one side of each boundary segment defines *material* (i.e. inside) and the other side defines *holes* (outside), as in figure 3.3. Material that overlaps material is simply material. Each hole is able to annihilate exactly one layer of material. Moreover, holes in space are ignored. It is

$$t \in P \iff f_{x_P}(t) > 0$$

For applications of this convention, see again [Newe80].

For polygons, another way of describing the oriented multiply-covered convention is to say that a point is considered to be inside the polygon if the *winding number* of the boundary with respect to that point is greater than zero. The winding number of a polygon boundary with respect to a given point is defined as the net number of times that a point on the boundary wraps around the given point while the boundary point makes one complete traversal of the boundary.

To eliminate some of the flaws of this convention, Newell and Sequin [Newe80] propose yet another convention, the so-called *nonzero winding number*

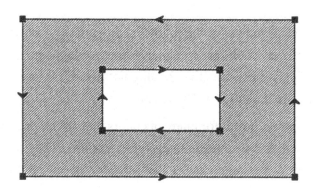

Figure 3.3: Oriented multiply-covered convention (from [Newe80]).

convention. According to this convention, a point is considered to be inside a polygon if the winding number of the boundary with respect to that point is nonzero (fig. 3.4). Using the notation of polyhedral chains, this approach can be generalized to arbitrary dimensions and described in a much simpler way. The winding number with respect to a point t is simply $f_{x_p}(t)$. According to the nonzero winding number convention, it is

$$t \in P \iff f_{x_p}(t) \neq 0$$

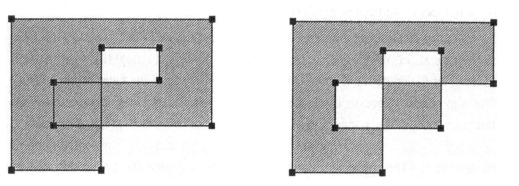

Figure 3.4: Nonzero winding number convention (from [Newe80]).

According to any of the above inside-outside conventions, all equivalent chains correspond to the same point set in E^d.

3.3. Properties

Polyhedral chains may have the following properties. A polyhedral chain x is called *disjoint* if its cells are mutually non-overlapping, and it is called *non-negative* if $f_x(t)$ is non-negative for all points $t \in E^d$. Moreover, a polyhedral chain is called *convex* if all of its cells are convex.

Disjoint chains are useful for many operators that are frequently performed on geometric data such as set operators or point locations. They are also useful to obtain the function f_x of some chain x, because for any disjoint chain $x = \sum_i \alpha_i p_i$, $f_x(t)$ is simply the coefficient α_k of the cell p_k, where $t \in p_k$. In order to transform an arbitrary polyhedral chain into an equivalent disjoint one, one may use the d-dimensional generalization of a plane sweep algorithm, similar to the one described in [Niev82]. The input to this algorithm is a map which is defined as a planar graph G embedded in the plane such that the edges of G intersect only at common vertices of G. If G is connected, it subdivides the plane into r simply connected internal regions $R_1 .. R_r$ and one external unbounded region R_0. In the algorithm, a straight line is swept across the map; during the sweep a data structure is dynamically maintained that keeps track of the regions that intersect the sweep line. This data structure is updated each time the sweep line encounters a vertex of G. The algorithm retrieves vertex lists of the polygonal regions $R_1 .. R_r$ in time $O(n \log n)$ where n is the number of vertices of graph G.

Our application requires the following modifications. First, the algorithm has to be generalized to d dimensions; this can be done in a straightforward manner. Second, let E denote the d-dimensional graph consisting of the faces of the cells p_i. The map graph G consists of the faces in E plus some extra faces to connect the different connected components of E. Hence, G is a connected graph. For each p_i intersecting the sweep hyperplane, the algorithm retrieves the corresponding coefficient α_i. The coefficient β_j corresponding to a region R_j is then obtained by adding the α_i that correspond to the cells containing R_j. The sweep data structure has to keep track not only of the R_j, but also of the coefficients β_j. With these modifications, the algorithm yields a disjoint polyhedral chain $\sum_j \beta_j R_j$, equivalent to the original chain $\sum_i \alpha_i p_i$.

In many cases, multiple layers or negative space are not needed, because one only distinguishes between the inside and the outside of a polyhedron. Applications like this are served well by non-negative polyhedral chains x where $f_x(t)$ is 0 for outside points and positive otherwise. Given some arbitrary, possibly self-intersecting polyhedron P, defined by a chain x_P, one may transform x_P into a non-negative chain as follows. First, x_P is transformed into an equivalent disjoint chain x_P', as described above. Then some inside-outside convention is chosen to map each coefficient of x_P' into either 1 or 0, depending on whether the corresponding cell is inside or outside P. P now corresponds to the union of the cells in x_P'.

Convex polyhedral chains also have important applications because the convex cells can be described in a very simple way as an intersection of halfspaces (see section 2.5.3). If the set C of convex cells to be represented is known and finite (as in the case of a geometric database), the representation scheme can be simplified even further. Let $\mathbf{H}$ be a vector of all hyperplanes that embed some face of some cell in C. Then each element of C can be represented by an $|\mathbf{H}|$-dimensional vector, consisting of 1's, 0's, and −1's. Each 1 or −1 selects a hyperplane from $\mathbf{H}$, and associates an orientation with it. The resulting set of halfspaces represents a convex polyhedron. This approach is conceptually simple, provides support for set operators, and seems well suited for parallel processing; it will be discussed in great detail in the following sections.

Any polyhedral chain can be transformed into an equivalent convex polyhedral chain by splitting all the cells in the chain into convex pieces. There are several efficient algorithms known to partition a given general polyhedron into disjoint convex components; see, for example, [Chaz84].

3.4. Convex Polyhedral Chains as Representation Scheme

Consider a database consisting of a collection of general d-dimensional polyhedra in Euclidean space $\mathbf{E}^d$. To support set and search operators, we propose to represent the polyhedra as convex, non-negative polyhedral chains, which we will also refer to as *convex chains*. Formally, each polyhedron P is represented as a convex chain in $\mathbf{E}^d$,

$$x_P = \sum_{i=1}^{m} p_i$$

The cells p_i are d-dimensional closed convex point sets that are not necessarily bounded. A point is inside P if and only if it is inside any of the cells p_i, i.e.

$t \in P \iff t \in p_i$ for some $i=1 \ldots m$

Note that we do not require the cells to be mutually disjoint. Disjointness is hard to maintain and provides no particular advantages for the operators we intend to support. Therefore, the cells p_i form a *convex cover* of the polyhedron P. Note also that for any polyhedral chain x in $\mathbf{E^d}$ and a given inside-outside convention, there is a convex chain x' in $\mathbf{E^d}$, such that x and x' represent the same polyhedral point set.

Unlike simple polyhedra, convex chains are closed under all set operators such as intersection (fig. 3.5).

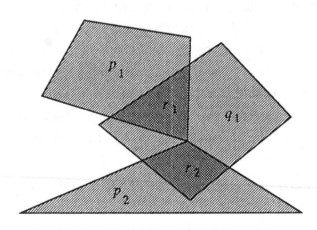

Figure 3.5: $x_P = p_1 + p_2$, $x_Q = q_1$, $x_{P \cap Q} = r_1 + r_2$

Convex chains can be viewed as a special case of the constructive solid geometry (CSG) approach proposed by Requicha [Requ80]. CSG represents a geometric object by a binary tree whose leaves correspond to geometric primitives and whose interior nodes correspond to set operators. In our case, the cells are the primitives, and all interior nodes correspond to the union operator. Like CSG, convex chains are a hierarchical representation scheme for polyhedra that is unambiguous, but not necessarily unique.

3.5. The h-Vector

The next question is how to represent the convex cells p_i. It is well known that any convex polyhedron in E^d is the intersection of closed halfspaces in E^d. Each halfspace in turn can be represented as a product $h \cdot H$ where H is an oriented $(d-1)$-dimensional hyperplane and h is an integer number. In particular, let $a \in E^d - \{0\}$ and $c \in E^1$; then the $(d-1)$-dimensional set $H(a,c) = \{x \in E^d : x \cdot a = c\}$ defines a hyperplane in E^d. A hyperplane $H(a,c)$ defines two closed halfspaces $1 \cdot H(a,c) = \{x \in E^d : x \cdot a \geq c\}$ and $-1 \cdot H(a,c) = \{x \in E^d : x \cdot a \leq c\}$. For completeness, we define $0 \cdot H(a,c)$ as E^d. A hyperplane H *supports* a convex cell p if $H \cap p \neq \phi$[†] and it is $p \subseteq 1 \cdot H$ or $p \subseteq -1 \cdot H$. If H is any hyperplane supporting p then $H \cap p$[†] is a *face* of p. The faces of dimension 1 are called *edges*; those of dimension 0 *vertices*. A supporting hyperplane H is called a *boundary* hyperplane is the face $H \cap p$[†] is of dimension $d-1$.

Let $\mathbf{H} = H_1 H_2 .. H_{|\mathbf{H}|}$ denote a vector of $(d-1)$-dimensional oriented hyperplanes such that H_i is in $\mathbf{H}$ if and only if H_i is a boundary hyperplane of some cell p in the database. For simplicity, we require that for each $(d-1)$-dimensional face f of any convex cell p there be a $(d-1)$-dimensional face g of a polyhedron P in the database, such that f and g are both subsets of the same hyperplane. Then $\mathbf{H}$ can be restricted to include only those hyperplanes that are boundary hyperplanes of some polyhedron P in the database.

Now each cell in the database can be represented as an $|\mathbf{H}|$-dimensional vector, consisting of 1's, 0's, and −1's. Each 1 or −1 selects a hyperplane from $\mathbf{H}$, and associates an orientation with it. The resulting set of halfspaces represents a convex polyhedron. More formally, each cell p is represented as a ternary vector $\mathbf{h}_p = \{0,1,-1\}^{|\mathbf{H}|}$, such that $p = \bigcap_{i=1}^{|\mathbf{H}|} (\mathbf{h}_p)_i \cdot H_i$. An example is given in figure 3.6.

Note that for a given cell p, $\mathbf{h}_p$ is by no means unique. For example, suppose that the hyperplane H_i is not a boundary hyperplane of cell p, but p is a subset of the halfspace $1 \cdot H_i$. Then it makes no difference whether $(\mathbf{h}_p)_i$ is 0 or 1; the hyperplane H_i is *redundant* with respect to p. For a given p, the set of all possible $\mathbf{h}_p$-

---

† Here the operator $\cap$ denotes the simple intersection operator and not the regularized one, as defined by Tilove [Tilo80].

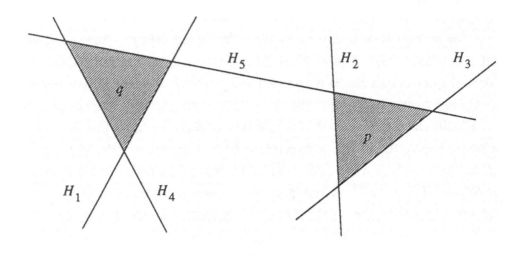

Figure 3.6: $\mathbf{h}_p=(0,1,-1,0,-1)$, $\mathbf{h}_q=(-1,0,0,1,-1)$

vectors is an equivalence class which contains a unique vector with the minimum number of nonzero components. For this unique minimum $\mathbf{h}_p$ every nonzero component corresponds to a boundary hyperplane of p. Note that there is no unique minimum vector to represent the empty set. On the other hand, there is a unique minimum vector to represent the whole space $\mathbf{E}^d$, viz., the vector $0^{|\mathbf{H}|}$.

The insertion of new polyhedra is performed by adding new hyperplanes to $\mathbf{H}$, if necessary. For simplicity we assume that the components of the ternary vectors $\mathbf{h}_p$ default to zero if they are not explicitly specified. Under this assumption an insertion does not change the representations of existing cells.

The deletion of polyhedra may cause some hyperplanes in $\mathbf{H}$ to become redundant with respect to all cells in the database. The deletion of such a hyperplane from $\mathbf{H}$ corresponds to a compression of each vector $\mathbf{h}_p$ by one component. Although it may not be efficient to perform this update after each single deletion, it might be worthwhile to do such a clean-up after a certain number of deletions. Otherwise a large number of redundant hyperplanes will inflate the representations unnecessarily.

It $\mathbf{H}$ contains many hyperplanes, as it may well be the case, the explicit storage representation of $\mathbf{h}_p$ is not feasible. However, the simple structure of $\mathbf{h}_p$ allows many alternative data structures to be used. As one example, $\mathbf{h}_p$ could be represented by a set of (signed) pointers, pointing to those hyperplanes that correspond to the nonzero elements.

Note that this approach to represent polyhedra abandons the notion of vertex completely. Representation of cells by h-vectors has both conceptual and computational advantages. To represent cells in terms of boundary hyperplanes rather than in terms of vertices is usually the most space-efficient way because no adjacency relations need to be stored. This becomes especially important in higher dimensions as the number of adjacencies may grow exponentially in the dimension; see [Prep85], pp. 89-93, or [Edel87], pp. 6-10. Furthermore, it seems that vertices are not necessary for the search and set operators we intend to support. Search operators such as point location or range search can be supported efficiently by search structures that are based on hyperplanes rather than vertices; examples for such structures are the binary space partitioning tree [Fuch80] or the cell tree (see chapter 5). All set operators can be computed efficiently without using vertices by decomposing them into two parts: (a) an operation on the h-vectors without references to the geometric coordinates of the hyperplanes, and (b) a generic operation that tests whether a vector $\mathbf{h}_p$ is *null*, i.e. whether the intersection of the halfspaces specified by $\mathbf{h}_p$ is empty. This decomposition will be described in detail in the following section.

3.6. Set Operators

Let P and Q be two general polyhedral point sets. We now show that the computation of any set operator on P and Q can be decomposed into: (a) operations on the corresponding h-vectors, and (b) deleting the null vectors from the set of resulting h-vectors. The following propositions are easily verified with the definitions of set operators and of polyhedral chains.

Proposition 3.1: Let P and Q be represented by convex chains $x_P = \sum\limits_{j=1}^{m} p_j$ and $x_Q = \sum\limits_{k=1}^{l} q_k$. Then

$$x_{P \cup Q} = x_P + x_Q$$

$$x_{P \cap Q} = \sum_{j,k} (p_j \cap q_k)$$

$$x_{\bar{P}} = x_{\bar{p}_1 \cap \cdots \cap \bar{p}_m}$$

$$x_{P-Q} = x_{P \cap \bar{Q}}$$

$\qquad\qquad\qquad\qquad\qquad\qquad\qquad\qquad\qquad\qquad\qquad$ $\square$

Proposition 3.2: Let $\mathbf{h}_p$ denote a h-vector of a cell p. Then $x_{\bar{p}} = -\mathbf{h}_p \cdot \mathbf{H}$. □

For an example see figure 3.7. Note that the length of this chain equals the number of nonzero components of the vector $\mathbf{h}_p$. It is therefore desirable to keep this number low, possibly at its minimum.

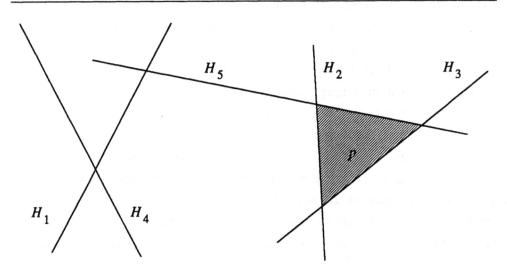

Figure 3.7: $\mathbf{h}_p = (0,1,-1,0,-1)$, $x_{\bar{p}} = -1 \cdot H_2 + 1 \cdot H_3 + 1 \cdot H_5$

Proposition 3.3: Let $\mathbf{h}_p$ and $\mathbf{h}_q$ denote the h-vectors for two cells p and q respectively. Then $\mathbf{h}_{p \cap q}$ can be computed using the following table for each component $(\mathbf{h}_{p \cap q})_i$. In those cases denoted by *, the hyperplane H_i separates p and q, i.e. $p \subseteq 1 \cdot H_i$ and $q \subseteq -1 \cdot H_i$, or vice versa, and therefore $p \cap q = \phi$.

$(\mathbf{h}_{p \cap q})_i$		$(\mathbf{h}_q)_i$		
		0	1	-1
	0	0	1	-1
$(\mathbf{h}_p)_i$	1	1	1	*
	-1	-1	*	-1

□

Note that both the intersection and the complementation operator are defined on the components of the h-vector. The components are independent of each other and can therefore be processed in parallel. In particular, a systolic array [Kung79] seems to be promising for an efficient implementation.

It follows from propositions 3.1-3.3 that for any set operation &, the h-vector representation of $P \& Q$ can be computed from the h-vector representations of P and Q. However, the h-vectors in the resulting representation may not be minimal. Also, some vectors may define empty sets, due to the fact that condition * is a sufficient, but not a necessary condition for non-intersection. Two cells p and q may not intersect, but there is no component $(\mathbf{h}_{p \cap q})_i$ where condition * occurs. In that case, the resulting vector $\mathbf{h}_{p \cap q}$ defines an empty set. Although that case is consistent with our data model, it is not desirable. A large number of empty cells p_j in the convex chains $x_P = \sum_{j=1}^{m} p_j$ representing the polyhedra in the database may slow down the system performance considerably. We therefore need an efficient means for detecting empty cells.

One approach would be to increase the number of nonzero components in the h-vector, possibly to its maximum, i.e.

$$(\mathbf{h}_p)_i = \begin{cases} 1 \text{ if } p \subseteq 1 \cdot H_i \\ -1 \text{ if } p \subseteq -1 \cdot H_i \\ 0 \text{ otherwise} \end{cases}$$

Each nonzero component increases the chance that a separating hyperplane is found, i.e. that condition * is met if two polyhedra do not intersect. If each h-vector had a maximum number of nonzero components then a separating hyperplane would be detected immediately; i.e. condition * would be a necessary and sufficient condition for non-intersection. On the other hand, this approach makes the identification of boundary hyperplanes and therefore the cell complementation and boundary retrieval operations much more difficult. Also, computing the above function for each cell p in the database requires an immense amount of computation and produces a lot of data that is probably never needed.

A garbage collector seems to be a better solution. Each time a new cell is computed as the intersection of two cells, the new cell is tagged. A background process (the garbage collector) keeps checking the tagged cells in the database for emptiness. If a cell is found non-empty, it is untagged. Otherwise, it is deleted from storage and from the chains that contain that cell. Unfortunately, the representation of cells by means of their **h**-vectors does not lead to an efficient algorithm to check cells for emptiness. A better approach to this problem, based on geometric duality, is presented in chapter 4 of this book. There we show that the time complexity to check two cells for intersection is polylogarithmic and therefore sublinear in the number of boundary hyperplanes of any of the cells.

In order to avoid duplicating computational effort and losing information, we propose to cache the results obtained by the garbage collector. Whenever a cell intersection $p \cap q$ is computed a second time, it should be immediately clear from the vectors $\mathbf{h}_p$ and $\mathbf{h}_q$ if the intersection $p \cap q$ is empty or not. Whenever the garbage collector checks a new cell $p \cap q$, it either discovers a separating hyperplane (if p and q are disjoint) or it discovers that there are no separating hyperplanes (if p and q intersect). This result can be cached by extending the notion of the **h**-vector to capture more information in the following way.

Given a cell p and a hyperplane H_i, there are two pieces of information about the relationship between p and H_i that are of interest and that should be cached in the component $(\mathbf{h}_p)_i$:

(i)   Which side of H_i is p on? Possible answers are: to the left (−1), to the right (+1), H_i intersects the interior of p (I), or unknown (0).

(ii) Is H_i a boundary hyperplane of p? Yes (Y), No (N), or unknown (0).

Clearly, if H_i intersects the interior of p then it can not be a boundary hyperplane of p. Also, if it is not known on which side of H_i p is on, then H_i must not be a boundary hyperplane; otherwise, p would not be defined properly. Hence, of the twelve possible combinations, only the following eight combinations make sense:

		side			
		1	−1	I	0
boundary hyperplane?	Y	ok	ok	-	-
	N	ok	ok	ok	ok
	0	ok	ok	-	-

Now each cell p is represented as a vector $\mathbf{h}_p^+$ with the following semantics. Each component is one of the following eight combinations:

$(\mathbf{h}_p^+)_i$	Meaning
$(1,Y)$	$p \subseteq 1 \cdot H_i$, H_i is a boundary hyperplane of p
$(-1,Y)$	$p \subseteq -1 \cdot H_i$, H_i is a boundary hyperplane of p
$(1,0)$	$p \subseteq 1 \cdot H_i$, H_i may or may not be a boundary hyperplane of p
$(-1,0)$	$p \subseteq -1 \cdot H_i$, H_i may or may not be a boundary hyperplane of p
$(1,N)$	$p \subseteq 1 \cdot H_i$, H_i is not a boundary hyperplane of p
$(-1,N)$	$p \subseteq -1 \cdot H_i$, H_i is not a boundary hyperplane of p
(I,N)	H_i intersects the interior of p
$(0,N)$	H_i is not a boundary hyperplane of p

Components that are not explicitly specified default to $(0,N)$. It turns out that these $\mathbf{h}_p^+$-vectors are closed with respect to intersection of two cells. $(\mathbf{h}_{p \cap q}^+)_i$ is given by the following table:

$(\mathbf{h}^+_{p\cap q})_i$		$(\mathbf{h}^+_q)_i$							
		$(1,Y)$	$(-1,Y)$	$(1,0)$	$(-1,0)$	$(1,N)$	$(-1,N)$	(I,N)	$(0,N)$
$(\mathbf{h}^+_p)_i$	$(1,Y)$	$(1,0)$	*	$(1,0)$	*	$(1,0)$	*	$(1,0)$	$(1,0)$†
	$(-1,Y)$	*	$(-1,0)$	*	$(-1,0)$	*	$(-1,0)$	$(-1,0)$	$(-1,0)$†
	$(1,0)$	$(1,0)$	*	$(1,0)$	*	$(1,0)$	*	$(1,0)$	$(1,0)$†
	$(-1,0)$	*	$(-1,0)$	*	$(-1,0)$	*	$(-1,0)$	$(-1,0)$	$(-1,0)$†
	$(1,N)$	$(1,0)$	*	$(1,0)$	*	$(1,N)$	*	$(1,N)$	$(1,N)$
	$(-1,N)$	*	$(-1,0)$	*	$(-1,0)$	*	$(-1,N)$	$(-1,N)$	$(-1,N)$
	(I,N)	$(1,0)$	$(-1,0)$	$(1,0)$	$(-1,0)$	$(1,N)$	$(-1,N)$	$(0,N)$	$(0,N)$
	$(0,N)$	$(1,0)$†	$(-1,0)$†	$(1,0)$†	$(-1,0)$†	$(1,N)$	$(-1,N)$	$(0,N)$	$(0,N)$

In those cases denoted by *, the hyperplane H_i separates p and q, i.e. $p \subseteq 1 \cdot H_i$ and $q \subseteq -1 \cdot H_i$, or vice versa. Therefore, a new cell $p \cap q$ is certainly empty if any component $(\mathbf{h}_{p \cap q})_i$ corresponds to one of the cases denoted by *. Otherwise, the hyperplane H_i *may* separate p and q if and only if $(\mathbf{h}_{p \cap q})_i$ corresponds to one of the cases denoted by †. Hence, the cell $p \cap q$ needs to be tagged if and only if there is at least one component $(\mathbf{h}_{p \cap q})_i$ that corresponds to one of the cases denoted by †. Then the garbage collector will check if the cell $p \cap q$ is in fact empty or not.

If a tagged cell $p \cap q$ is found empty, this result can be cached by the following updates. Let H_i be a separating hyperplane and, w.l.o.g. let $p \subseteq 1 \cdot H_i$ and $q \subseteq -1 \cdot H_i$.

IF $(\mathbf{h}^+_p)_i = (0,N)$
THEN $(\mathbf{h}^+_p)_i := (1,N)$
IF $(\mathbf{h}^+_q)_i = (0,N)$
THEN $(\mathbf{h}^+_q)_i := (-1,N)$

If, on the other hand, a tagged cell $p \cap q$ is found non-empty, this result can be cached as follows. There are no separating hyperplanes between p and q, i.e. for any hyperplane H_i that may be a boundary hyperplane of p, either (a) q lies on the same side of H_i as p, or (b) H_i intersects the interior of q. A similar condition holds for any hyperplane H_i that may be a boundary hyperplane of q. Therefore,

IF $((\mathbf{h}_p^+)_i = (\pm 1, Y)$ OR $(\mathbf{h}_p^+)_i = (\pm 1, 0))$ AND $(\mathbf{h}_q^+)_i = (0, N)$
THEN IF $H_i \cap q = \phi$ THEN $(\mathbf{h}_q^+)_i := (\pm 1, N)$
ELSE $(\mathbf{h}_q^+)_i := (I, N)$

IF $((\mathbf{h}_q^+)_i = (\pm 1, Y)$ OR $(\mathbf{h}_q^+)_i = (\pm 1, 0))$ AND $(\mathbf{h}_p^+)_i = (0, N)$
THEN IF $H_i \cap p = \phi$ THEN $(\mathbf{h}_p^+)_i := (\pm 1, N)$
ELSE $(\mathbf{h}_p^+)_i := (I, N)$

Whenever $p \cap q$ is computed again, it follows from the vectors $\mathbf{h}_p^+$ and $\mathbf{h}_q^+$ if p and q intersect or not. If they do intersect, the intersection cell will not have to be tagged again.

When a new cell is inserted into the database, most of the components of its $\mathbf{h}^+$-vector are $(0, N)$. As set operations are performed on the stored polyhedra, the database evolves. More and more $(0, N)$ components of the $\mathbf{h}^+$-vectors are replaced, and the vectors carry more and more information. Therefore, it will happen less and less frequently that a new cell has to be tagged and checked for emptiness. Also, at some point it may be more efficient to test a new cell $p \cap q$ for emptiness by checking the hyperplanes that may be separating ones (i.e. the ones that correspond to one of the cases denoted by †) one by one if they are actually separating. If the number of such hyperplanes is sufficiently small, this may be simpler and faster than using the dual approach proposed in chapter 4.

Problems such as complementation, point location or boundary retrieval may be solved by looking at only those hyperplanes that may be boundary hyperplanes, i.e. the hyperplanes H_i where $(\mathbf{h}_p^+)_i$ is $(\pm 1, Y)$ or $(\pm 1, 0)$.

There are variations to this approach. First, one may prefer to always identify the boundary hyperplanes of each cell, i.e. to avoid vector components $(\pm 1, 0)$. This can be achieved by extending the garbage collector, such that each time an intersection cell is found non-empty, its boundary hyperplanes are computed and the $\mathbf{h}^+$-vector is updated accordingly. Second, one may decide to simplify the update procedure above by introducing additional aggregation states $(1I, N)$ and $(-1I, N)$ which represent $(1, N)$ OR (I, N) and $(-1, N)$ OR (I, N), respectively. Then the set of updates for the case that p and q intersect can be simplified to

IF $((\mathbf{h}_p^+)_i = (\pm 1, Y)$ OR $(\mathbf{h}_p^+)_i = (\pm 1, 0))$ AND $(\mathbf{h}_q^+)_i = (0, N)$
THEN $(\mathbf{h}_q^+)_i := (\pm 1I, N)$

IF $((\mathbf{h}_q^+)_i = (\pm 1, Y)$ OR $(\mathbf{h}_q^+)_i = (\pm 1, 0))$ AND $(\mathbf{h}_p^+)_i = (0, N)$
THEN $(\mathbf{h}_p^+)_i := (\pm 1I, N)$

In particular, it is not necessary anymore to check any hyperplane H_i that is a boundary hyperplane of p (q) if it intersects the interior of q (p), i.e. if $H_i \cap q = \phi$ ($H_i \cap p = \phi$). It still follows from the new vectors $\mathbf{h}_p^+$ and $\mathbf{h}_q^+$ if p and q intersect or not. If they do intersect, the intersection cell will not have to be tagged again. As proven in chapter 4, the time complexity to check the condition $H_i \cap q = \phi$ ($H_i \cap p = \phi$) for a particular hyperplane H_i is logarithmic in the number of boundary hyperplanes of q (p).

3.7. Summary

We introduced the concept of polyhedral chains as a representation scheme for polyhedra in arbitrary dimensions, and presented in detail a scheme that is based on convex chains. Our scheme is conceptually simple, facilitates the efficient computation of set operators, and seems well suited for parallel processing. Each cell is represented as an intersection of halfspaces, encoded in a vector. The notion of vertices is abandoned completely as it is not needed for the set and search operators we intend to support.

Based on this representation, we described a scheme to decompose the computation of set operators into two steps. The first step consists of a collection of vector operations; the second step is a garbage collection where those vectors are eliminated that represent empty cells. All results of the garbage collection are cached in the vectors in such a way that no computations have to be duplicated. As the database is learning more and more information through the garbage collector, it will be able to detect empty cells immediately such that no additional test for emptiness is required. No special treatment of singular intersection cases is needed. This approach to set operations is significantly different from algorithms that have been proposed in the past: it makes no use of vertices, edges, or adjacencies, it does not induce a space partitioning to localize the set operations, and it is applicable to polyhedra in arbitrary dimensions.

Chapter 4

A Dual Approach to Detect Polyhedral

Intersections in Arbitrary Dimensions

4.1. Introduction

In the previous chapter, we encountered the problem of detecting the intersection of two convex cells. A fast solution to this problem directly affects the efficiency of the garbage collector, which in turn has a direct impact on the efficiency of the h-vector representation scheme as a whole. Detecting and computing intersections is a fundamental problem in computational geometry [Lee84]. Fast solutions for intersection problems are desirable in a wide range of application areas, including linear programming [Dant63], hidden surface elimination [Newm79], or geometric databases. In many of these applications, the dimension of the intersection problems may be greater than three. This is particularly obvious in linear programming; another example are database applications where geometric objects are used to represent predicates [Ston86b].

It was first noted by Chazelle and Dobkin [Chaz80] that it is often easier to *detect* the intersection of two suitably preprocessed geometric objects rather than to actually *compute* it. In the detection problem, one only asks if two objects intersect or not; also, it is allowed to preprocess each of the given objects separately.

In this chapter, which is an extended version of [Gunt87b], we present algorithms to solve the intersection detection problem in arbitrary dimensions for hyperplanes and convex polyhedra. A *(d-dimensional, convex) polyhedron P* in d-dimensional Euclidean space $\mathbf{E^d}$ is defined to be the intersection of some finite number of closed halfspaces in $\mathbf{E^d}$, such that the dimension of the smallest affine subspace containing P is d. As in chapter 3, we say that a hyperplane $H(a,c) = \{x \in \mathbf{E^d} : x \cdot a = c\}$ $(a \in \mathbf{E^d} - \{0\}, c \in \mathbf{E^1})$ supports a polyhedron P if $H(a,c) \cap P \neq \phi$ and $P \subseteq 1 \cdot H(a,c)$. If $H(a,c)$ is any hyperplane supporting P then $H(a,c) \cap P$ is a *face* of P. The faces of dimension 1 are called *edges*; those of dimension 0 *vertices*. A supporting hyperplane is called a *boundary* hyperplane if the face $H(a,c) \cap P$ is of dimension $d-1$. The faces of P that are a subset of some supporting hyperplane $H(a,c)$, with $a_d \leq 0$, form the *upper hull* of P. Similarly, the faces with $a_d \geq 0$ form the *lower hull* of P.

So far, the intersection detection problem has only been considered in two and three dimensions. In their original paper, Chazelle and Dobkin [Chaz80] solve the d-dimensional hyperplane-polyhedron intersection problem in time $O(\log n)$ $(d=2)$ and $O(\log^2 n)$ $(d=3)$, and the polyhedron-polyhedron intersection problem in time $O(\log n)$ $(d=2)$ and $O(\log^3 n)$ $(d=3)$. Here, n denotes the maximum number of vertices of any given polyhedron. Both problems require $O(n)$ $(d=2)$ and $O(n^2)$ $(d=3)$ space and preprocessing. A revised version of that paper has been published recently [Chaz87]. In the three-dimensional case, $O(n \log n)$ space and preprocessing are also sufficient [Dobk80], in which case the running times given above have to be multiplied by a $\log n$ factor.

In a later paper, Dobkin and Kirkpatrick [Dobk83] improve the running times of Chazelle and Dobkin for the three-dimensional case by a factor of $\log n$. The new upper bounds are $O(\log n)$ and $O(\log^2 n)$ for the hyperplane-polyhedron and the polyhedron-polyhedron problems, respectively. As the algorithms of Chazelle and Dobkin, their algorithms require $O(n^2)$ storage and preprocessing. Again, the results of Dobkin and Munro [Dobk80] can be used to reduce the space and preprocessing requirements in three dimensions to $O(n \log n)$, in which case the running times increase by a $\log n$ factor.

In d dimensions, we obtain upper time bounds of $O(2^d \log n)$ to detect the intersection of a hyperplane and a polyhedron, and $O((2d)^{d-1} \log^{d-1} n)$ to detect the intersection of two polyhedra. These time bounds are the first results of their kind for $d > 3$; they match the time bounds given by Dobkin and Kirkpatrick [Dobk83] for $d=2$ and $d=3$. Furthermore, our results seem to be the first of their kind that extend to unbounded polyhedra as well.

We obtain our results by means of a geometric duality transformation in d-dimensional Euclidean space $\mathbf{E}^d$ that is an isomorphism between points and hyperplanes [Prep79, Brow79, Lee84, Edel87]. Each convex polyhedron P is represented by a set of two functions in the dual space, $TOP^P, BOT^P : \mathbf{E}^{d-1} \to \mathbf{E}^1$, such that a hyperplane H intersects P if and only if the dual of H lies between TOP^P and BOT^P. Then, two polyhedra P and Q intersect if and only if for all $x \in \mathbf{E}^{d-1}$, we have $TOP^P(x) \geq BOT^Q(x)$ and $TOP^Q(x) \geq BOT^P(x)$.

For $d=2$ and for the hyperplane-polyhedron intersection problem in $d=3$, the space and preprocessing requirements of the dual representation scheme are $O(n)$ and therefore optimal. For the three-dimensional hyperplane-polyhedron intersection problem, this represents an improvement over the results of Dobkin and Kirkpatrick [Dobk83] by a factor of n. The three-dimensional polyhedron-polyhedron problem takes quadratic space and preprocessing, as does the algorithm of Dobkin and Kirkpatrick.

For general d, the scheme requires $O(n^{2^d})$ space and preprocessing. To improve these bounds is a subject of further research. In particular, we suspect that lower bounds may be achieved at the expense of slightly higher time bounds for the detection algorithms (see also section 4.6).

Section 4.2 introduces the dual representation scheme for convex polyhedra. Sections 4.3 and 4.4 show how the hyperplane-polyhedron and the polyhedron-polyhedron intersection detection problems can be solved efficiently using the dual scheme. Section 4.5 presents several extensions of our approach, and section 4.6 contains our conclusions.

4.2. The Dual Representation Scheme

If the hyperplane $H(a,c)$ is non-vertical (i.e. $a_d \neq 0$), then H intersects the d-th coordinate axis in a unique and finite point and can be represented by an equation

$$x_d = b_1 x_1 + \ldots + b_{d-1} x_{d-1} + b_d$$

where $b_i = -a_i / a_d$ ($i = 1 \ldots d-1$) and $b_d = c$. F_H denotes the function whose graph is H, i.e.

$$F_H : E^{d-1} \rightarrow E^1$$
$$F_H(x_1 \ldots x_{d-1}) = b_1 x_1 + \ldots + b_{d-1} x_{d-1} + b_d.$$

A point $p = (p_1 \ldots p_d)$ lies *above* (*on*, *below*) H if $p_d > (=,<) F_H(p_1 \ldots p_{d-1})$.

Brown [Brow79] defines a duality transformation D in E^d that maps hyperplanes into points and vice versa. The dual $D(H)$ of hyperplane H is the point $(b_1 \ldots b_d)$ in E^d. Conversely, the dual $D(p)$ of a point p is the hyperplane defined by the equation

$$x_d = -p_1 x_1 - p_2 x_2 - \cdots - p_{d-1} x_{d-1} + p_d.$$

Lemma 4.1: A point p lies above (on, below) a hyperplane H if and only if the dual $D(H)$ lies below (on, above) $D(p)$.

Proof: Let H be given by the equation $F_H(x_1 \ldots x_{d-1}) = b_1 x_1 + \ldots + b_{d-1} x_{d-1} + b_d$ and let $p = (p_1 \ldots p_d)$ be a point above (on, below) H, i.e.

$$p_d > (=,<) F_H(p_1 \ldots p_{d-1}) \quad (*).$$

Inserting $D(H) = (b_1 \ldots b_d)$ into $F_{D(p)}$ yields

$$F_{D(p)}(b_1 \ldots b_{d-1}) = -p_1 b_1 - \ldots - p_{d-1} b_{d-1} + p_d > (=,<) b_d \quad \text{(due to (*))}$$

Hence, $D(p)$ lies below (on, above) $D(H)$. □

A hyperplane H intersects a bounded polyhedron P if and only if there are two vertices v and w of P such that H lies between v and w (i.e. v lies on or above H and w lies on or below H, or vice versa). According to lemma 4.1, this is the case if and only if the dual $D(H)$ lies between the duals $D(v)$ and $D(w)$.

This observation leads to a new representation scheme for bounded convex polyhedra. Consider the functions $TOP^P, BOT^P : E^{d-1} \to E^1$ that are defined for a convex polyhedron P as follows. Here, V_P denotes the set of vertices of P.

$$TOP^P(x_1 \ldots x_{d-1}) = \max_{v \in V_P} F_{D(v)}(x_1 \ldots x_{d-1})$$

$$BOT^P(x_1 \ldots x_{d-1}) = \min_{v \in V_P} F_{D(v)}(x_1 \ldots x_{d-1})$$

Obviously, both functions are piecewise linear, continuous, and TOP^P is convex, whereas BOT^P is concave [Rock70]. With this notation, a non-vertical hyperplane H intersects P if and only if $D(H)$ lies between TOP^P and BOT^P. More formally, the hyperplane H, given by the equation $x_d = b_1 x_1 + \ldots + b_{d-1} x_{d-1} + b_d$, intersects P if and only if $BOT^P(b_1 \ldots b_{d-1}) \leq b_d \leq TOP^P(b_1 \ldots b_{d-1})$. A two-dimensional example of a polyhedron P and the corresponding functions TOP^P and BOT^P is given in figure 4.1.

It is easily possible to extend this representation scheme to unbounded polyhedra. For simplicity, however, the main part of this paper is restricted to bounded polyhedra; the case of unbounded polyhedra is discussed in more detail in section 4.5.1.

The two functions TOP^P and BOT^P can be viewed as a mapping that map any slope $(b_1 \ldots b_{d-1})$ of a non-vertical hyperplane into the maximum (TOP^P) or

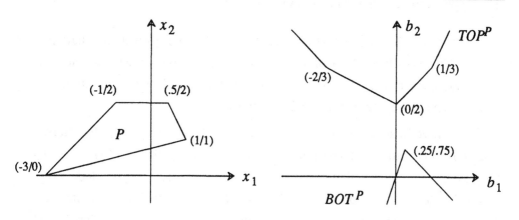

Figure 4.1

minimum (BOT^P) intercept b_d such that the hyperplane given by $x_d = b_1 x_1 + \ldots + b_{d-1} x_{d-1} + b_d$ intersects the polyhedron. We have

Theorem 4.2: Each convex polyhedron P corresponds to exactly one pair of functions (TOP^P, BOT^P), and conversely.

Proof : The functions TOP^P and BOT^P are uniquely defined for any convex regular polyhedron P, i.e. there is only one pair of functions (TOP^P, BOT^P) for any P.

Conversely, suppose there were two convex polyhedra P and Q such that $P \neq Q$, but $TOP^P(x_1 \ldots x_{d-1}) = TOP^Q(x_1 \ldots x_{d-1})$ and $BOT^P(x_1 \ldots x_{d-1}) = BOT^Q(x_1 \ldots x_{d-1})$ for all $(x_1 \ldots x_{d-1}) \in \mathbf{E}^{d-1}$.

Case 1: $P \cap Q = \phi$. Then there exists a non-vertical separating hyperplane H such that all points of P lie above H and all points of Q lie below H, or vice versa. There also exists a hyperplane H' parallel to H that intersects P. H' does not intersect Q. I.e., the dual $D(H')$ lies between TOP^P and BOT^P, but not between TOP^Q and BOT^Q. This is a contradiction to our assumption.

Case 2: $P \cap Q \neq \phi$. Because of $P \neq Q$ it is $P - Q \neq \phi$ or $Q - P \neq \phi$. W.l.o.g., let $P - Q \neq \phi$. Let p be some interior point of $P - Q$. There exists a non-vertical separating hyperplane H such that all points of Q lie above H and point p lies below H, or vice versa. There also exists a hyperplane H' parallel to H that goes through p. Because of $p \in P$, H' intersects P, but it does not intersect Q. Contradiction to our assumption as above. $\qquad \square$

4.3. Hyperplane-Polyhedron Intersection Detection

For simplicity of presentation, we assume that the given hyperplane is non-vertical. This can always be achieved by a suitable rotation of the coordinate system. It is also possible to extend our detection algorithm to detect intersections with a vertical hyperplane; see section 4.5.2 for details.

A non-vertical hyperplane H, given by $x_d = b_1 x_1 + \ldots + b_{d-1} x_{d-1} + b_d$ intersects a bounded polyhedron P if and only if $BOT^P(b_1 \ldots b_{d-1}) \leq b_d \leq TOP^P(b_1 \ldots b_{d-1})$. Moreover, an intersecting hyperplane H supports P if and only if $b_d = BOT^P(b_1 \ldots b_{d-1})$ or $b_d = TOP^P(b_1 \ldots b_{d-1})$. Therefore, the intersection detection problem can be solved by obtaining the functional values $TOP^P(b_1 \ldots b_{d-1})$ and $BOT^P(b_1 \ldots b_{d-1})$. It follows from the definition of TOP^P and BOT^P that these values can be found in time $O(d \cdot n)$ by computing $F_{D(v)}(b_1 \ldots b_{d-1})$ for each vertex $v \in V_P$. With some preprocessing, however, one can obtain logarithmic time bounds as follows.

It follows from [Brow79] that there is the following isomorphism between the upper hull of the polyhedron P and the graph of TOP^P. Each k-dimensional face f of the upper hull of P corresponds to exactly one $(d-k-1)$-dimensional face $D(f)$ of TOP^P's graph, and vice versa. Furthermore, if two faces f_1 and f_2 of P's upper hull are adjacent, then so are the faces $D(f_1)$ and $D(f_2)$ of TOP^P's graph. The same isomorphism exists between P's lower hull and the graph of BOT^P. Hence, the graphs of TOP^P and BOT^P are polyhedral surfaces in E^d, consisting of no more than n convex $(d-1)$-dimensional faces and no more than $m = O(n^2)$ $(d-2)$-dimensional faces.

Without loss of generality, we only show how to obtain $TOP^P(b_1 \ldots b_{d-1})$. The projection of TOP^P's graph on the $(d-1)$-dimensional hyperplane $J : b_d = 0$ subdivides J into no more than n convex $(d-1)$-dimensional polyhedral partitions with no more than m $(d-2)$-dimensional boundary segments. Any given partition $E \subseteq J$ corresponds to a vertex $v(E)$ of P's upper hull, such that for any point $(p_1 \ldots p_{d-1}) \in E$, it is $TOP^P(p_1 \ldots p_{d-1}) = F_{D(v(E))}(p_1 \ldots p_{d-1})$. Hence, $TOP^P(b_1 \ldots b_{d-1})$ can be obtained by a $(d-1)$-dimensional point location in J to find the partition E that contains the point $(b_1 \ldots b_{d-1})$, followed by a computation of $F_{D(v(E))}(b_1 \ldots b_{d-1})$.

For $d=2$ and $d=3$, the computation of $F_{D(v(E))}(b_1 \ldots b_{d-1})$ takes only constant time. The point location can be performed in time $O(\log n)$, using the algorithm of Edelsbrunner, Guibas, and Stolfi [Edel86a] for point location in a monotone subdivision. The total time complexity to detect the intersection of a hyperplane and a polyhedron is therefore $O(\log n)$. The space and preprocessing requirements are only $O(n)$, due to the fact that, in our case, the given partitions are convex and therefore monotone.

For general d, it takes time $O(d)$ to compute the functional value $F_{D(v(E))}(b_1 \ldots b_{d-1})$. Dobkin and Lipton [Dobk76] solve a $(d-1)$-dimensional point location problem with m $(d-2)$-dimensional boundary segments recursively as follows. In a preprocessing step, they compute the $O(m^2)$ $(d-3)$-dimensional intersection segments formed by the m original boundary segments, and project them on some $(d-2)$-dimensional hyperplane K. This way, the point location problem can be solved by a point location problem in K, followed by a binary search of the m original segments. Therefore, the time complexity of the point location is

$$TPL(d-1,m)$$

$$\leq TPL(d-2,m^2) + (d-1)(\lfloor \log m \rfloor + 1)$$

$$\leq \ldots$$

$$\leq TPL(2,m^{2^{d-3}}) + \sum_{i=1}^{d-3} (d-i)(\lfloor 2^{i-1} \log m \rfloor + 1)$$

$$= O(2^d \log m)$$

$$= O(2^d \log n)$$

We obtain a total time complexity of $O(2^d \log n)$.

For general d, the space requirements of the dual algorithm are as follows. The equations of the $O(n)$ faces require space $O(dn)$. The space requirements to store a convex subdivision of $\mathbf{E}^2$ with m boundary segments, $SP(2,m)$, is $O(m)$ [Edel86a]. For a subdivision of $\mathbf{E}^{d-1}$ with m boundary segments, one has to store a subdivision of the $(d-2)$-dimensional projection hyperplane K with m^2 boundary segments and a sequence of no more than m boundary segments for each of the partitions. The number of partitions is no more than $m^{2(d-2)}$ [Edel86b]. Therefore,

$$SP\,(d-1,m)$$

$$\leq SP\,(d-2,m^2) + m^{2(d-2)}m$$

$$\leq SP\,(d-3,m^4) + m^{4(d-3)}m^2 + m^{2(d-2)}m$$

$$\leq \ldots$$

$$\leq SP\,(2,m^{2^{d-3}}) + O\,(m^{2^{d-1}})$$

$$= O\,(m^{2^{d-1}})$$

$$= O\,(n^{2^d})\,.$$

We obtain a total space complexity of $O\,(n^{2^d})$.

The preprocessing requirements of this algorithm are as follows. Each $(d-2)$-dimensional boundary segment of the subdivision is obtained from the original polyhedron P in time $O\,(d)$ by dualization and projection. Here, we assume that P is given by a list of its faces and the corresponding adjacency relations. As there are $m = O\,(n^2)$ $(d-2)$-dimensional boundary segments, it takes time $O\,(dn^2)$ to obtain all of them.

The preprocessing requirements to solve a point location problem in a convex subdivision of $\mathbf{E}^2$ with m boundary segments, $PRP\,(2,m)$, are $O\,(m)$ [Edel86a]. For a subdivision of $\mathbf{E}^{d-1}$ with m boundary segments, one has to compute m^2 intersections, and to project them on some $(d-2)$-dimensional hyperplane K. For each of the at most $m^{2(d-2)}$ partitions, one has to sort the $O\,(m)$ boundary segments. Finally, one has to do the necessary preprocessing for the subdivision of K. Therefore,

$$PRP\,(d-1,m)$$

$$\leq PRP\,(d-2,m^2) + m^{2(d-2)}m\log m$$

$$\leq PRP\,(d-3,m^4) + m^{4(d-3)}m^2\log m^2 + m^{2(d-2)}m\log m$$

$$\leq \ldots$$

$$\leq PRP\,(2,m^{2^{d-3}}) + O\,(m^{2^{d-1}})$$

$$= O\,(m^{2^{d-1}})$$

$$= O\,(n^{2^d})\,.$$

We obtain a total preprocessing time of $O\,(n^{2^d})$. Theorem 4.3 summarizes our results for the hyperplane-polyhedron intersection detection problem.

Theorem 4.3: Given a non-vertical $(d-1)$-dimensional hyperplane H and a d-dimensional convex polyhedron P, H and P can be tested for intersection in time $T(d,n)$ with $S(d,n)$ space and $PP(d,n)$ preprocessing:

$P \cap H = \emptyset$?	$T(d,n)$	$S(d,n)$	$PP(d,n)$
$d=2$	$O(\log n)$	$O(n)$	$O(n)$
$d=3$	$O(\log n)$	$O(n)$	$O(n)$
$d>3$	$O(2^d \log n)$	$O(n^{2^d})$	$O(n^{2^d})$

Proof : follows from the preceding discussion. $\square$

4.4. Polyhedron-Polyhedron Intersection Detection

Two convex polyhedra P and Q do not intersect if and only if there is a separating non-vertical hyperplane between them. Any such hyperplane H does not intersect either P or Q, but there are hyperplanes H' and H'' parallel to H, such that H' is above H and H'' is below H, and either H' intersects P and H'' intersects Q, or vice versa. More formally, a non-vertical hyperplane H, given by the equation $x_d = b_1 x_1 + \ldots + b_{d-1} x_{d-1} + b_d$, separates the polyhedra P and Q if and only if

$$TOP^P(b_1 \ldots b_{d-1}) < b_d < BOT^Q(b_1 \ldots b_{d-1}), \text{ or}$$

$$TOP^Q(b_1 \ldots b_{d-1}) < b_d < BOT^P(b_1 \ldots b_{d-1}).$$

Therefore, two polyhedra P and Q intersect if and only if[*]

(i) $\displaystyle\min_{(x_1 .. x_{d-1}) \in E^{d-1}} (TOP^P - BOT^Q)(x_1 \ldots x_{d-1}) \geq 0$, and

(ii) $\displaystyle\min_{(x_1 .. x_{d-1}) \in E^{d-1}} (TOP^Q - BOT^P)(x_1 \ldots x_{d-1}) \geq 0$.

See figure 4.2 for two examples. If both conditions are only met as equalities, then only the boundaries of P and Q intersect, but not their interiors.

With the definitions of TOP^P and BOT^P, these conditions form a linear programming problem with no more than $2n$ constraints. According to Megiddo [Megi84], the time complexity to solve this problem is bound by $2^{O(2^d)} \cdot 2n$. Hence,

---

[*] We write $(f \pm g)(x)$ for $f(x) \pm g(x)$.

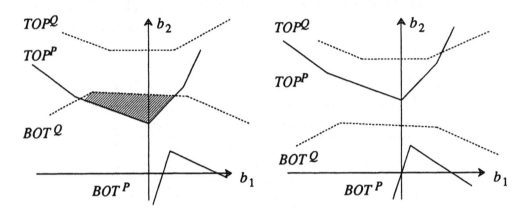

(a) no intersection: the points in the shaded area are the duals of the separating hyperplanes.

(b) intersection

Figure 4.2

the conditions can be tested in linear time $O(n)$ if the dimension is fixed. With some preprocessing, however, the conditions can be tested in polylogarithmic time as follows.

Without loss of generality, we only show how to test condition (i). We present a multidimensional search technique that finds the minimum of a convex piecewise linear function in arbitrary dimensions. The technique is recursive; it solves a d-dimensional problem by solving $O(d\log n)$ $(d-1)$-dimensional problems, and so on.

In the two-dimensional case, condition (i) can be tested by a variation of Dobkin and Kirkpatrick's algorithm [Dobk83] to detect the intersection of two polygons. The graphs of TOP^P and BOT^Q are monotone convex polygonal chains with edges $t_1 .. t_k$ and $u_1 .. u_l$ $(k+l \leq 2n)$; see also figure 4.1. The relative position and the slopes of the edges $t_{\lfloor k/2 \rfloor}$ and $u_{\lfloor l/2 \rfloor}$ give enough information to eliminate half of the edges of one (or both) chains from further consideration without missing the minimum. The algorithm proceeds recursively, eliminating at least one quarter of the remaining edges at each recursion level. Therefore, the minimum is detected in time $O(\log n)$ without any preprocessing or extra space. A similar analysis yields the same bound to test condition (ii).

In order to solve the d-dimensional problem, we solve $O(d\log n)$ $(d-1)$-dimensional problems. It is well known [Dant63] that the global minimum of $TOP^P - BOT^Q$ occurs at some vertex of the graph of $TOP^P - BOT^Q$, i.e. at some vertex $M=(M_1 \ldots M_d)$ of TOP^P's graph TG or BOT^Q's graph BG. Let $(v_1 \ldots v_{|TG|})$ denote the sequence of vertices in V_{TG}, sorted by increasing x_1-coordinate. We consider the vertex $v_{\lfloor |TG|/2 \rfloor}$ and its x_1-coordinate $\overline{b}_1$, and compute the local minimum of $TOP^P - BOT^Q$ along the hyperplane $x_1 = \overline{b}_1$. This is a $(d-1)$-dimensional minimization problem and can be solved recursively; let $m=(m_1=\overline{b}_1, m_2 \ldots m_d)$ denote some point where the local minimum is assumed. Due to the convexity of $TOP^P - BOT^Q$, we can determine the position of M relative to m from the local slope of $TOP^P - BOT^Q$. We have

Lemma 4.4: It is $M_1 > (<) m_1$ if and only if there is an $\varepsilon_0 > 0$, such that for all ε with $0 < \varepsilon < \varepsilon_0$

$$(TOP^P - BOT^Q)(m_1 - \varepsilon, m_2 \ldots m_d)$$
$$>(<) \quad (TOP^P - BOT^Q)(m_1 \ldots m_d)$$
$$>(<) \quad (TOP^P - BOT^Q)(m_1 + \varepsilon, m_2 \ldots m_d).$$

Otherwise, m is a global minimum of $TOP^P - BOT^Q$.

Proof : Due to the convexity of the function $TOP^P - BOT^Q$, there is always an $\varepsilon_0 > 0$, such that for all ε with $0 < \varepsilon < \varepsilon_0$ exactly one of the following conditions holds:

(i) $(TOP^P - BOT^Q)(m_1 - \varepsilon, m_2 \ldots m_d) > (TOP^P - BOT^Q)(m_1 \ldots m_d)$
$> (TOP^P - BOT^Q)(m_1 + \varepsilon, m_2 \ldots m_d)$

(ii) $(TOP^P - BOT^Q)(m_1 - \varepsilon, m_2 \ldots m_d) < (TOP^P - BOT^Q)(m_1 \ldots m_d)$
$< (TOP^P - BOT^Q)(m_1 + \varepsilon, m_2 \ldots m_d)$

(iii) $(TOP^P - BOT^Q)(m_1 - \varepsilon, m_2 \ldots m_d) \geq (TOP^P - BOT^Q)(m_1 \ldots m_d)$
$\wedge \ (TOP^P - BOT^Q)(m_1 + \varepsilon, m_2 \ldots m_d) \geq (TOP^P - BOT^Q)(m_1 \ldots m_d)$

If condition (iii) holds, then m is a local minimum. Because $TOP^P - BOT^Q$ is convex, m also has to be a global minimum. Conversely, if m is a global minimum, condition (iii) clearly has to be true.

We now show indirectly that $M_1 > m_1$ implies condition (i). Suppose that $M_1 > m_1$, but (i) does not hold. Because m is not a global minimum, condition (ii) has to be true. Let $r = (r_1, r_2 = m_2, r_3 \ldots r_d)$ denote the minimum of $TOP^P - BOT^Q$ along the hyperplane $x_2 = m_2$. Due to (ii) and to the convexity of $TOP^P - BOT^Q$, it is $r_1 < m_1$ and $r_d < m_d$. Therefore, the line segment (M, r) intersects the hyperplane

$x_1=m_1$ in some point $s = (s_1=m_1, s_2 .. s_d)$. Because of $M_d \leq r_d$, it is $s_d \leq r_d$, and because of $r_d < m_d$, it is $s_d < m_d$. This is a contradiction, because s lies on the hyperplane $x_1=m_1$, and m is the minimum along this hyperplane. A two-dimensional example is given in figure 4.3.

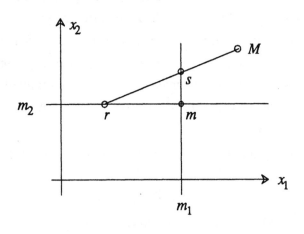

Figure 4.3

Hence, $M_1 > m_1$ implies condition (i). Similarly, it can be shown that $M_1 < m_1$ implies condition (ii). Due to the mutual exclusiveness of conditions (i), (ii) and (iii), we obtain that (i) implies $M_1 > m_1$ and so on. This proves the lemma. □

Therefore, looking up the functional values $(TOP^P - BOT^Q)(m_1 \pm \varepsilon, m_2 .. m_d)$ for some suitable $\varepsilon > 0$ gives us enough information to eliminate half of the vertices in V_{TG} (and some vertices in V_{BG}) from the search without missing the global minimum. If the search among the vertices in TG does not yield a global minimum, one continues with a similar search among the remaining vertices of BG. Hence the global minimum is obtained in no more than $\log(|TG|) + \log(|BG|)$ iterations.

The analysis of this algorithm obviously depends on the cardinalities of TG and BG. A simple combinatorial analysis shows that at any recursion level it is $|TG| + |BG| \leq n^d$, i.e. the algorithm requires no more than $2d \log n$ iterations. Each iteration involves a $(d-1)$-dimensional minimization and the four function lookups necessary to obtain $(TOP^P - BOT^Q)(m_1 \pm \varepsilon, m_2 .. m_d)$. As shown in section 4.3, each lookup can be carried out in no more than $2^{d+2} \log n$ steps. We obtain a total time complexity

$$T(d,n)$$

$$\leq 2d\log n \cdot (4 \cdot 2^{d+2}\log n + T(d-1,n))$$

$$\leq 2d\log n \cdot (4 \cdot 2^{d+2}\log n + 2(d-1)\log n \cdot (4 \cdot 2^{d+1}\log n + T(d-2,n)))$$

$$\leq \ldots$$

$$\leq \sum_{i=2}^{d-1} 2^{d+5} d^{i-1}\log^i n$$

$$= O((2d)^{d-1}\log^{d-1} n).$$

Of course, in practice one might be able to solve the intersection detection problem much faster by checking at various stages if $(TOP^P - BOT^Q)(x_1 \ldots x_{d-1}) < 0$, or $(TOP^Q - BOT^P)(x_1 \ldots x_{d-1}) < 0$.

For $d=3$, the space and preprocessing requirements of this algorithm are as follows. The equations of the $O(n)$ faces of P and Q require space $O(n)$. For the multidimensional binary search one has to store (a) a subdivision of the x_1-axis into no more than $n+1$ partitions, and (b) a sequence of $O(n)$ boundary segments for each one of the partitions. The total space requirements are therefore $O(n^2)$. The preprocessing can be done in time $O(n^2)$ by means of a plane sweep as described in [Prep85], pp. 47-48.

For $d>3$, the data structures required to do the search are essentially the same as the ones required to do the point location as described in section 4.3. Therefore, the space and preprocessing requirements are the same as for the hyperplane-polyhedron intersection detection problem. We obtain

Theorem 4.5: Given two d-dimensional convex polyhedra P and Q, P and Q can be tested for intersection in time $T(d,n)$ with $S(d,n)$ space and $PP(d,n)$ preprocessing:

$P \cap Q = \phi$?	$T(d,n)$	$S(d,n)$	$PP(d,n)$
$d=2$	$O(\log n)$	$O(n)$	$O(n)$
$d=3$	$O(\log^2 n)$	$O(n^2)$	$O(n^2)$
$d>3$	$O((2d)^{d-1}\log^{d-1} n)$	$O(n^{2^d})$	$O(n^{2^d})$

Proof : follows from the preceding discussion.   □

4.5. Extensions

4.5.1. Unbounded Polyhedra

Clearly, there exist functions TOP^P and BOT^P for an unbounded polyhedron P, such that a hyperplane H intersects P if and only if the dual $D(H)$ lies between TOP^P and BOT^P. The question is how to define these functions in a way that allows to construct their graphs easily by dualization of the original polyhedron P. In the case of bounded polyhedra, we base our definition on the notion of vertex, which is obviously not sufficient for the unbounded case. One simple way to generalize our definitions of TOP^P and BOT^P,

$$TOP^P(x_1 \ldots x_{d-1}) = \max_{v \in V_P} F_{D(v)}(x_1 \ldots x_{d-1})$$

$$BOT^P(x_1 \ldots x_{d-1}) = \min_{v \in V_P} F_{D(v)}(x_1 \ldots x_{d-1})$$

to an unbounded polyhedron P, is to enhance V_P by some *virtual* vertices at infinity. In particular, let C_P denote a d-dimensional cube with edge length $E(C_P)$ that contains all vertices of P. The bounded polyhedron $P \cap C_P$ has a set of vertices $V_{P \cap C_P} = V_P \cup \bar{V}$, where $\bar{V}$ contains those vertices that are formed by intersections of C_P with edges of P. As $E(C_P)$ goes to infinity, so do the vertices in $\bar{V}$. The dual $D(\bar{v})$ of any vertex $\bar{v} \in \bar{V}$ goes towards a vertical hyperplane with a corresponding function $F_{D(\bar{v})}: E^{d-1} \to \pm\infty$. Now the functions $TOP^P, BOT^P: E^{d-1} \to E^1 \cup \{\pm\infty\}$ are defined as

$$TOP^P(x_1 \ldots x_{d-1}) = \lim_{E(C_P) \to \infty} \max_{v \in V_P \cup \bar{V}} F_{D(v)}(x_1 \ldots x_{d-1})$$

$$BOT^P(x_1 \ldots x_{d-1}) = \lim_{E(C_P) \to \infty} \min_{v \in V_P \cup \bar{V}} F_{D(v)}(x_1 \ldots x_{d-1})$$

Again, there is an isomorphism between the upper hull of P and the graph of TOP^P, as well as between the lower hull of P and the graph of BOT^P [Brow79]. Note that the virtual vertices are only a conceptual aid. They do not have to be taken into account when constructing the graphs by dualization. If the dual of P's upper hull does not yield a finite value $b_d = TOP^P(b_1 \ldots b_{d-1})$ for some $(b_1 \ldots b_{d-1}) \in E^{d-1}$, then the functional value at $(b_1 \ldots b_{d-1})$ is assumed $+\infty$. Similarly, the default for $BOT^P(b_1 \ldots b_{d-1})$ is $-\infty$. The algorithms to detect intersections do not have to be modified, except for the possibility that TOP^P and BOT^P may now assume the values $\pm\infty$. A two-dimensional example is given in figure 4.4.

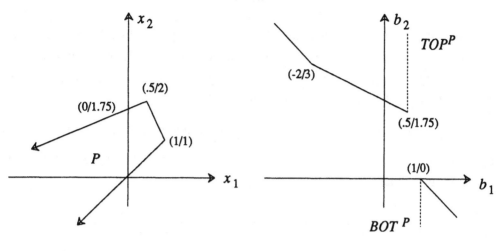

Figure 4.4

4.5.2. Vertical Hyperplanes

Vertical hyperplanes pose a problem for the dual scheme because they do not have a dual point with finite coordinates. However, for each vertical hyperplane H there is a virtual dual point at infinity. Let (H_n) denote a sequence of non-vertical hyperplanes that converges towards H, such that all hyperplanes H_n have the same $(d-2)$-dimensional point set Q in common (i.e. Q is the intersection of any two hyperplanes H_{n_1} and H_{n_2}).

Let $F_{H_n}(x_1 .. x_{d-1}) = b_1^n x_1 + .. + b_{d-1}^n x_{d-1} + b_d^n$. As described in section 4.3, $TOP^P(b_1^n .. b_{d-1}^n)$ is obtained as follows. First, one performs a $(d-1)$-dimensional point location in the projection of TOP^P's graph on the hyperplane $J: b_d = 0$ to find the partition $E \subseteq J$ that contains the point $(b_1^n .. b_{d-1}^n)$. Then, one computes the functional value $F_{D(v(E))}(b_1^n .. b_{d-1}^n)$, where $v(E)$ is the vertex of P that corresponds to the partition E.

Lemma 4.6: There is an $n_0 \in \mathbf{N}$ such that for all $n > n_0$ all duals $D(H_n)$ belong to the same partition $\bar{E} \subseteq J$.

Proof: Because Q is a subset of each hyperplane H_n, each dual point $D(H_n)$ lies on the dual non-vertical straight line $D(Q)$. Clearly, $(D(H_n))$ goes to infinity as n goes to infinity. On the other hand, each partition $E \subseteq J$ is convex, and the number of partitions is finite. From there, the lemma follows. □

In order to check H for intersection with some polyhedron P, one can now proceed similarly as in the case of a non-vertical hyperplane. The partition $\bar{E}$ can be obtained by a point location. Then, one computes the two limits

$$\lim_{n \to \infty} (TOP^P (b_1^n \mathrel{..} b_{d-1}^n) - F_{D(v(\bar{E}))}(b_1^n \mathrel{..} b_{d-1}^n)) \qquad \text{and}$$

$$\lim_{n \to \infty} (F_{D(v(\bar{E}))}(b_1^n \mathrel{..} b_{d-1}^n) - BOT^P (b_1^n \mathrel{..} b_{d-1}^n)).$$ H intersects P if and only if both

limits are greater or equal zero. Moreover, H supports P if and only if at least one of the limits is finite.

4.6. Summary

We showed that in arbitrary, but fixed dimensions, the hyperplane-polyhedron and the polyhedron-polyhedron intersection detection problems can be solved in logarithmic and polylogarithmic time, respectively. For dimensions larger than three, these results are the first of their kind. There are two reasons why, as of now, these results are of primarily theoretical interest. First, the coefficient which is exponential in d becomes prohibitively high for higher dimensions. Second, the space and preprocessing requirements are not suitable for practical purposes. It is subject to further research to improve these results in order to achieve practical algorithms for intersection detection in higher dimensions. In particular, we suspect that lower bounds for space and preprocessing may be achieved at the expense of slightly higher time bounds for the detection algorithms.

Note: After this work has been completed, Meiser [Meis88] presented a new point location algorithm based on Clarkson's work on random sampling [Clar87]. This algorithm can be used to solve the hyperplane-polyhedron intersection detection problem in dual space in time $O(d^5 \log n)$ with $O(n^{d+\kappa})$ space and $O(n^{d+1+\kappa'})$ preprocessing for arbitrary $\kappa, \kappa' > 0$.

Chapter 5

The Cell Tree:

An Index for Geometric Databases

5.1. Introduction

In this chapter, we discuss search operators and suitable geometric index structures to support them. Given a set of geometric objects in d-dimensional Euclidean space $\mathbf{E}^d$, stored in a geometric database, a *range search* computes those objects in the database that overlap a given search space $S \subset \mathbf{E}^d$. In the *point search* problem, which can be viewed as a degenerate range search, one determines all objects in the database that contain a given point $A \in \mathbf{E}^d$. Both operators require fast access to objects in the database, depending on their location in space. Therefore geometric index structures can be used efficiently to support these operators.

Indices for the computation of (one-dimensional) search operators play an important role in conventional database systems [Baye72, Come79]. Indices should be dynamic with respect to updates of the database, i.e. it should be possible to perform insertions and deletions without having to reorganize the index completely. Furthermore, an index should minimize the number of page faults that occur during a search operation.

Section 5.2 gives a brief survey of the most well-known data structures and indices for the support of geometric search operators. Section 5.3 reviews convex chains, which serve as a representation scheme in the geometric database used in this chapter. Section 5.4 introduces an index for this database, viz., a new hierarchical data structure termed *cell tree*, and describes how to perform search operations. Section 5.5 gives algorithms to perform insertions and deletions on the cell tree, and section 5.6 summarizes this chapter.

5.2. Geometric Index Structures

There is a whole variety of well-known data structures for the computation of geometric search operators. *Quadtrees* [Fink74, Same84] are designed to organize two-dimensional data. The decomposition process starts from a square that contains all objects to be represented, and proceeds with a recursive subdivision into four equal-sized quadrants. Corresponding to this subdivision is a tree structure of degree four (the quadtree), i.e. each node has exactly four descendants. See chapter 2 for a more detailed description. Due to the regular decomposition, quadtrees do not adapt to the distribution of the data objects in space nor to changes in the underlying database. Objects whose boundaries do not fit into the rectilinear partition of the quadtree can only be represented approximately, or in form of an object description attached to the leaves of the quadtree. A further disadvantage of the region quadtree is that it does not take paging of secondary memory into account. In general, each node required during a search may cause a page fault. As quadtrees may be very deep, the paging costs incurred this way may be considerable. If quadtrees are generalized to higher dimensions, the branching factor is 2^d for d dimensions. At some point nodes will stretch over several pages which may also decrease the tree performance significantly.

Binary space partitioning (BSP) trees [Fuch80, Fuch83] are binary trees that represent a recursive subdivision of a given space into subspaces by means of $(d-1)$-dimensional hyperplanes. Each subspace is subdivided independent of its history and of the other subspaces. Each hyperplane corresponds to an interior node of the tree, and each partition corresponds to a leaf. Figure 5.1 gives an example of a BSP and the corresponding BSP tree. BSP trees are much more adaptive than quadtrees. However, they are typically very deep which has a negative impact on tree performance. They also do not account for paging of secondary memory.

Polygon trees [Will82] are an interesting data structure to perform polygon retrieval, which can be stated as follows. Given a set of n points in the plane and a general polygon, find the subset of these points lying inside the polygon. If the points are organized in a polygon tree, this problem can be solved in time $O(n^{\log_6 4})$ and space $O(n)$. As the BSP tree, the polygon tree corresponds to a partition of the plane into disjoint regions. It can be dynamized by means of standard dynamization techniques such as [Bent80], such that insertions and deletions of points can be interleaved with queries and no periodic reorganization is required. However, there is no obvious generalization of the polygon tree to higher dimensions or to extended geometric objects (rather than points). Also, polygon trees do not account for paging of secondary memory.

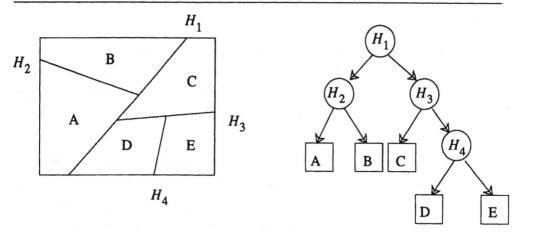

Figure 5.1: A binary space partitioning with BSP tree.

The first geometric index structure that has been designed specifically for paged memory is Robinson's *k-d-B-tree* [Robi81], a generalization of Bayer's B-tree [Baye72] to higher dimensions. k-d-B trees are designed for indexing points in arbitrary dimensions; a generalization to extended geometric objects (such as polyhedra) is not possible. The same restriction holds for three non-hierarchical point indices: Tamminen's *EXCELL* [Tamm82], Nievergelt's *gridfile* [Niev84], and for a hash-based access method designed by Kriegel and Seeger [Krie86]. All these index structures are dynamic, i.e. insertions and deletions of objects can be interleaved with searches and no periodic reorganization is required.

A direct generalization of these point index structures to handle extended objects is not possible. However, there are approaches to use these structures for extended objects. If the objects are d-dimensional intervals (*boxes*) they can be represented as points in $2d$-dimensional space (the *point space*) [Hinr85]. Then the search operators can be formulated as point queries in point space and computed by means of a point index. This method has several disadvantages. First, the images of two intervals that are nearby in original space may be arbitrarily far apart from each other in point space [Falo87]. Second, the images of intervals are distributed unevenly in point space (in particular, there are no images below the main diagonal, see [Falo87]). Third, the formulation of range queries in point space is much more complicated than it is in the original space. A recent analysis uses the example of the k-d-B-tree to demonstrate that these problems do in fact cause serious performance penalties [Gree88].

A more promising approach has been proposed by Six and Widmayer [Six86]. It can not only be used for the management of d-dimensional intervals, but for arbitrary extended d-dimensional geometric objects. The objects are indexed by means of a *layering* of several point indices. Six and Widmayer use a three-layer gridfile to demonstrate the advantages of their approach.

There are also several index structures that have been designed a priori as secondary storage indices for extended objects. The first such structure was Guttman's *R-tree* [Gutt84], also a generalization of the B-tree to higher dimensions. R-trees are balanced trees that correspond to a nesting of d-dimensional intervals (fig. 5.2). Each node N corresponds to a disk page $D(N)$ and an interval $I(N)$. If N is an interior node then all intervals corresponding to the immediate descendants of N are subsets of $I(N)$ and stored on the disk page $D(N)$. If N is a leaf node then $D(N)$ also contains a number of intervals that are subsets of $I(N)$. Each of these *data intervals* is wrapped tightly around a data object. For data objects that are not intervals themselves, the R-tree can therefore not solve a given search problem completely. One rather obtains a set of intervals whose enclosed objects *may* intersect the search space. One is left with the problem of testing the *objects* for intersection with the search space. This step, which may cause additional page faults and considerable computations, has not been taken into account by existing performance analyses [Gutt84, Gree88].

As in the case of the B-tree, there is an upper and lower bound for the number of descendants of an interior node. The lower bound prevents the degeneration of trees and leads to an efficient storage utilization. Nodes whose number of descendants drops below the lower bound are deleted and its descendants are distributed among the remaining nodes (*tree condensation*). The upper bound can be derived from the fact that each tree node corresponds to exactly one disk page. Once a node requires more than one disk page, it is split and its descendants are distributed among the two resulting nodes. Each splitting may propagate up the tree, i.e. it may be necessary to split the ancestor node as well, and so on.

Furthermore, it should be noted that sibling nodes, i.e. nodes whose ancestor nodes are identical, may correspond to overlapping intervals. This property of the R-tree facilitates the insertion and deletion of data objects, but it may lead to performance losses during search operations. In the case of point locations, one may have

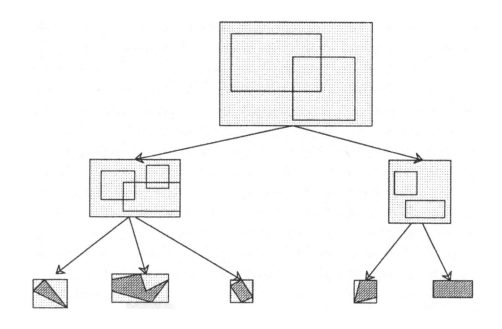

Figure 5.2: An R-tree with data objects (shaded).

to traverse several search paths. Even for range searches, the number of nodes to be inspected tends to be higher with overlaps. Moreover, the overlap tends to increase as objects are inserted into the R-tree [Gunt88]. These problems led to the development of techniques to minimize the overlap [Rous85] and to the R^+–tree [Ston86b, Sell87] where no overlaps are allowed (see fig. 5.3).

For the reasons mentioned above, the R^+-tree allows the fast computation of search operators. However, the insertion and deletion of data objects may be much more complicated in turn.

First, the insertion of an object O or its data interval I_O may require the enlargement of *several* sibling intervals (i.e. intervals corresponding to sibling nodes). This is especially (but not exclusively) the case if I_O overlaps several sibling intervals (see fig. 5.4). Each of these enlargements may require a considerable effort because it is always necessary to test for possible overlaps with sibling intervals. I_O is inserted into all corresponding subtrees; the insertion may therefore cause the creation of several leaf entries. In the R-tree, on the other hand, no more than one

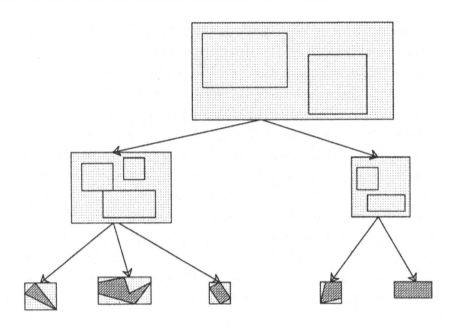

Figure 5.3: An R$^+$-tree with data objects (shaded).

interval per tree level will be enlarged; possible overlaps that result from the enlargement do not matter. Consequently, each insertion into an R-tree causes the creation of exactly one additional leaf entry.

Second, there are situations where the enlargement step *inevitably* leads to overlaps (see fig. 5.5). In this case, it is necessary to split one or more sibling intervals *before* the enlargements can take place.

Third, node splittings have to be propagated not only up the tree (as in the case of the R-tree) but also down the tree. The splitting of an interior node N corresponds to a splitting of the corresponding interval $I(N)$ by means of a hyperplane H. If there are intervals corresponding to descendant nodes of N that intersect H, then these intervals have to be split along H as well, and so on. It is therefore necessary to pick H very carefully to avoid complicated node splittings.

Fourth, it is no more possible to maintain an upper bound on the number of leaf node entries, i.e. there may be leaves that require more than one disk page of storage space. In particular, this is inevitable if there is a point in space that is

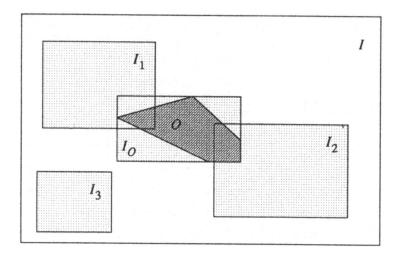

Figure 5.4: The data interval I_0 overlaps the sibling intervals I_1 and I_2. In this case I_0 has to be inserted into both corresponding subtrees. I_1 and I_2 have to be enlarged in such a way that $I_0 \subset I_1 \cup I_2$ (without I_1 overlapping I_2!).

covered by more data intervals than what can be stored on one disk page. The interval covering that point certainly contains too many data intervals for one disk page. To avoid complex update algorithms, the R^+-tree does not impose any upper or lower bounds on the number of descendants of an interior node. The degeneration of an R^+-tree is therefore possible, and storage utilization may deteriorate.

The main goal during the design of the *cell tree* was to facilitate searches on data objects of arbitrary shapes, i.e. especially on data objects which are not intervals themselves. Especially in robotics and computer vision, intervals are not necessarily a good approximation of the data objects enclosed. Now each tree node corresponds not necessarily to an interval, but to a convex polyhedron. In order to minimize the number of page faults, the leaf nodes of a cell tree contain all the information necessary to answer a given search query. No pages other than those containing the cell tree will be required. This is an important advantage of the cell tree over the R-tree and related structures, where data objects may have to be retrieved from memory, thereby causing additional page faults. To optimize search performance, we decided to avoid overlaps between sibling polyhedra. In subsequent

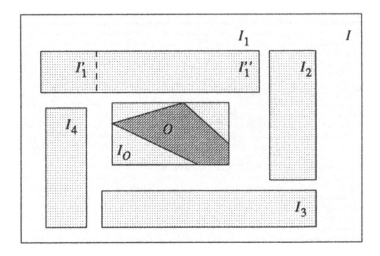

Figure 5.5: Here it is not possible to enlarge the sibling intervals $I_1 \ldots I_4$ in such a way that $I_0 \subset I_1 \cup \ldots \cup I_4$ without creating overlaps. It is therefore necessary to split one of the intervals, say I_1, into two subintervals I_1' and I_1'' before the enlargement can take place.

---

sections, it will be shown how the resulting disadvantages can be partly compensated by restricting the polyhedra to be partitions of a BSP (binary space partitioning) (see fig. 5.1). Therefore the cell tree can be viewed as a combination of a BSP- and an R^+-tree.

5.3. The Geometric Database

Consider a database consisting of a collection of d-dimensional point sets in Euclidean space $\mathbf{E^d}$. In order to support search and set operations efficiently, we use the scheme presented in chapter 3 and represent the data objects as convex chains, i.e. as sums of convex cells. Formally, each data object D is represented as a convex chain in $\mathbf{E^d}$,

$$x_D = \sum_{k=1}^{m} p_i$$

The cells p_i are d-dimensional convex closed point sets that are not necessarily bounded. Note that we do not require the cells to be mutually disjoint; the cells form a convex cover of the data object.

A point $t \in \mathbf{E^d}$ is considered inside D if and only if it is inside any of the cells, i.e. $t \in D \iff t \in p_i$ for some $i=1 .. m$

Note that the decomposition of the data objects into cells is completely transparent to the user. Cells need not be seen or manipulated by the user.

5.4. The Cell Tree

5.4.1. Description

A cell tree indexes the cells in a geometric database depending on their location in space. As the R-tree, a cell tree is a height-balanced tree and each tree node corresponds to exactly one disk page. The computation of a search operator should therefore cause only a small number of page faults. The cell tree is a fully dynamic index structure; insertions and deletions can be interleaved with searches and no periodic reorganization is required.

Each leaf node entry E represents a cell $E.Z$. In addition to a description of the cell geometry, it contains the ID $E.D$ of the data object whose convex chain $x_{E.D}$ contains the cell $E.Z$. E also contains any additional properties of the data object $E.D$ that may be necessary to answer a given query. Examples for such properties are the color or the geometry of $E.D$.

Interior (non-leaf) nodes contain entries of the form

$$(cp, P, C)$$

Here, cp is the child pointer, i.e. the address of the corresponding descendant node. P is a convex, not necessarily bounded d-dimensional polyhedron. All cells in the database that are subsets of P are in the subtree under the descendant node. C is a convex subset of P, which also contains each cell p in the subtree, i.e. $p \subseteq C$. C provides a more accurate localization of these cells, which may speed up search queries. In the following, $E.cp$, $E.P$, and $E.C$ denote the corresponding attributes of an interior node entry E. m is a parameter specifying the minimum number of entries in an interior node. Finally, given a node N, its entry in its ancestor node is denoted by E_N, and the entries in N are denoted by $E_i(N)$.

A cell tree satisfies the following properties.

(1) The root node has at least two entries unless it is a leaf.

(2) Each interior node has at least m entries unless it is the root.

(3) For each entry (cp, P, C) in an interior node, the subtree that cp points to contains a cell p if and only if $p \subseteq P$.

(4) For each entry (cp, P, C) in an interior node, $C \subseteq P$ is a convex polyhedron that can be specified as the intersection of P with at most k halfspaces in $\mathbf{E}^d$. For each cell p in the subtree pointed to by cp, it is $p \subseteq C$.

(5) For each interior node N, the polyhedra $E_i(N).P$ form a binary space partitioning (BSP) of $E_N.P$.

(6) All leaves are on the same level.

(7) Almost every node requires no more than one disk page of storage space.

Figure 5.6 shows an example cell tree.

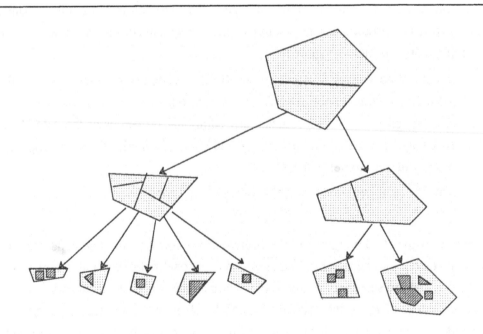

Figure 5.6: A cell tree with cells (shaded) for $m=2$. For simplicity, the polyhedra $E.C$ are omitted.

Property (5) has two interesting consequences. First, the polyhedra $E_1.P$ and $E_2.P$ corresponding to two entries E_1 and E_2 on the same tree level cannot overlap. Second, the entries of an interior tree node N can now be stored in a very compact manner: rather than describing the polyhedra $E_i(N).P$ explicitly, one only stores the BSP of $E_N.P$.

Note that the cell tree (just as the R^+-tree) does not put any upper bounds on the number of node entries. Nevertheless it is attempted to limit the storage requirements for each node to one disk page. If a node exceeds one disk page of storage after one or more insertions, it is attempted to split that node. In most cases this is in fact possible; see section 5.5.3. If the splitting does not succeed then the node is stored using overflow pages; these cases are the only ones that the word *almost* in property (7) refers to.

Other than the R^+-tree, however, the cell tree has a *lower* bound for the number of entries of an *interior* node. Of course, it is also possible to define the cell tree with a lower bound for the number of *leaf* entries. To keep insertions and deletions simple, however, we have decided not to impose such a bound.

In order to analyze the maximum number M of entries of an interior node N, such that the node can still be stored on one disk page, we denote the page size by ps, and the number of bytes required to store a number or a pointer by q. Each interior node entry $E_i(N)$ requires q bytes for the pointer $E_i(N).cp$, and $k \cdot d \cdot q$ bytes for those k $(d-1)$-dimensional hyperplanes that specify $E_i(N).C$ if $E_i(N).P$ is known. The polyhedra $E_i(N).P$ form a BSP of $E_N.P$ with no more than M partitions. Therefore, the corresponding BSP-tree requires the storage of no more than $M-1$ hyperplanes and $2M-2$ pointers. The total number of bytes to store a full interior node is therefore

$$M \cdot (q + k \cdot d \cdot q) + (M-1) \cdot d \cdot q + (2 \cdot M - 2) \cdot q$$
$$= \quad q \cdot (M \cdot ((k+1) \cdot d + 3) - d - 2)$$

As one node corresponds to one disk page of ps bytes, we obtain

$$M = \left\lfloor \frac{ps/q + d + 2}{(k+1) \cdot d + 3} \right\rfloor$$

For a typical set of parameters, such as $ps=1024$, $q=4$, $d=2$, and $k=2$, one obtains $M=28$.

A similar analysis for the maximum number of leaf node entries is not possible as the storage requirements per leaf node entry E may vary considerably, depending on the complexity of the cell $E.Z$.

The height of a cell tree containing n index records is bound by $\lfloor \log_m n \rfloor + 1$, because the branching factor of each node is at least m. The maximum number of nodes is $n + \left\lfloor \dfrac{n}{m} \right\rfloor + \left\lfloor \dfrac{n}{m^2} \right\rfloor + \left\lfloor \dfrac{n}{m^3} \right\rfloor + \ldots + 1$. Except for the root and for overloaded nodes, the worst-case space utilization is m/M for interior nodes.

If a new data object is inserted into the database, one first computes a convex cover of the object. Each convex component is then inserted into the cell tree. The number of components per data object is highly data-dependent. If all data objects are convex (as it is actually the case for CAD layout data, for example), of course there would be only one component per data object.

Note that the insertion of a convex component into the cell tree may cause the creation of *several* leaf node entries (i.e. cells). This is a general property of index structures based on a partitioning of space into non-overlapping components. As confirmed by empirical results [Fuch83, Gunt88], the average number of cells is usually no more than twice the number of components. However, this number is highly data-dependent. In exceptional cases, where there was a lot of overlap between objects in the database, three or four cells per component have been observed.

The parameters m and k are to be varied as part of the performance tuning. A large m will increase the space efficiency and decrease the height of the tree, which might in turn improve the search performance. On the other hand, a large m may cause updates to become very expensive, as tree condensations will occur more frequently and become more complex (see section 5.5.4). Initial tests indicate that m should be chosen small, i.e. $m=2$ or $m=3$ [Gunt88].

A large value for k allows a more accurate localization of the cells in a subtree, which might improve the search performance. On the other hand, k and M are inversely proportional. A large k will therefore yield a small M. This might in turn increase the tree height and decrease the search performance. Furthermore, a large k makes updates more complicated.

5.4.2. Searching

The cell tree allows efficient searches such as to find all data objects that over-lap a search space, where the search space may be of arbitrary shape. We give the algorithm for this search problem; other searches can be implemented by variations of this algorithm.

The search algorithm first computes a convex cover of the search space. For each convex component, the search algorithm descends the tree from the root in a manner similar to a B-tree or an R-tree. At each interior node, the search space is decomposed further into several disjoint convex subspaces, and a not necessarily convex remainder space. The remainder space is insignificant to the search and therefore eliminated. The convex subspaces are each passed to one of the subtreees to be decomposed recursively in the same manner. Note that this algorithm differs from the equivalent R-tree algorithm where the subspaces are allowed to overlap, thereby decreasing the search efficiency.

Algorithm **Search**(T,S). Given a cell tree with root node T, find all data objects that overlap a search space S.

S1. [Decompose S.] If S is not convex, find a (small) set of convex polyhedra S_i such that $\sum_i S_i = S$. For each S_i, **Search**(T,S_i) and stop.

S2. [Search subtree.] If T is not a leaf, check each entry $E_i(T)$ to determine whether $E_i(T).C$ overlaps S. If yes, **Search**$(T',S \cap E_i(T).C)$ where T' denotes the node $E_i(T).cp$ points to.

S3. [Search leaf node.] If T is a leaf, check each entry $E_i(T)$ to determine whether the cell $E_i(T).Z$ overlaps S. If yes, return the data object $E_i(T).D$.

Other than step S1, the main effort in this algorithm is to detect and compute overlaps between the search range S on one hand and the convex polyhedra $E_i(T).C$ or the cells $E_i(T).Z$ on the other hand. A very efficient method to perform these computations is based on the dual representation scheme presented in chapter 4. Using this representation for the search range, the polyhedra $E_i(T).C$ and the cells, the time complexity per entry for steps S2 and S3 is not much higher than in the case of the R- or R$^+$-tree [Gunt88].

5.5. Updating the Cell Tree

5.5.1. Insertion

To insert a new data object, one first computes a convex cover of the object. Then each component in the cover is inserted separately into the cell tree. Note that the insertion of *one* component may cause the creation of more than one new leaf node entries (i.e. cells). Inserting index records for new cells is similar to insertion into a B- or R-tree. Index records are added to the leaves, nodes that overflow are split, and splits propagate up the tree (see section 5.5.3).

Algorithm **InsertObject**(T,D). Insert a new data object D into a cell tree with root node T.

IO1. [Decompose D.] Find a (small) set of convex polyhedra D_i such that $\sum_i D_i = D$. For each D_i, **InsertComponent**(T, D, D_i).

Algorithm **InsertComponent**(T,D,D_i). Insert a component D_i of the data object D into the cell tree with root node T.

IC1. [Insert into subtree.] If T is not a leaf, check each entry $E_i(T)$ to determine whether $E_i(T).P$ overlaps D_i. If yes, expand $E_i(T).C$ to include $D_i \cap E_i(T).P$, and **InsertComponent**(T', D, $D_i \cap E_i(T).P$), where T' is the node $E_i(T).cp$ points to.

IC2. [Insert into leaf node.] If T is a leaf node, insert a new entry E into T where $E.D=D$ and $E.Z=D_i$. If T cannot be stored on one disk page anymore, **SplitLeaf**(T).

5.5.2. Deletion

In order to delete a data object D from a cell tree that indexes the object, one also first computes a convex cover of D. For each component D_i in the cover, a deletion step is performed. To avoid empty leaves, a tree condensation is performed where necessary (see section 5.5.4).

Algorithm **DeleteObject**(T,D). Delete the data object D from the cell tree with root node T.

DO1. [Decompose D.] If D is not convex, find a (small) set of convex polyhedra D_i such that $\sum_i D_i = D$. For each D_i, **DeleteComponent**(T, D, D_i).

DO2. [Condense tree.] For each leaf node LN that is marked, **CondenseTree**(LN).

Algorithm **DeleteComponent**(T,D,D_i). Delete the component D_i of the data object D from the cell tree with root node T.

CD1. [Search subtree.] If T is not a leaf, check each entry $E_i(T)$ whether $E_i(T).P$ overlaps D_i. If yes, **DeleteComponent**(T', D, $D_i \cap E_i(T).P$), where T' denotes the node $E_i(T).cp$ points to.

CD2. [Update leaf node.] If T is a leaf node, check each entry $E_i(T)$ whether $E_i(T).D = D$. If yes, remove the entry $E_i(T)$ from T. If T is now empty, mark T, otherwise contract $E_T.C$ if possible.

5.5.3. Node Splitting

As mentioned, it is attempted to store each leaf on no more than one disk page. If a leaf requires more storage space, it is attempted to split the leaf (and the cells it contains) in such a way that both subleaves can be stored on one disk page each. This is not always possible. An efficient algorithm to obtain a suitable splitting hyperplane is based on the plane sweep paradigm [Prep85]. One sweeps across the cells in the leaf node along l different directions. If this leads to a suitable splitting hyperplane, the leaf is split. In this case, the ancestor node may have to be split as well, and so on. If the split does not succeed, the leaf is stored using overflow pages. The parameter l is to be varied as part of the performance tuning. A large l will cause the splitting operation to be more costly, but it may yield a better hyperplane. We obtain the following algorithm.

Algorithm **SplitLeaf(***LN***)**. Given an overloaded leaf node LN in a cell tree, split LN along a hyperplane, and propagate the split up the tree if necessary.

SL1. [Find hyperplane.] Sweep across LN in l different directions, looking for a splitting hyperplane such that both subleaves can be stored on one disk page. If that does not succeed, stop. Otherwise let H_1 and H_2 denote the two disjoint halfspaces that are defined by the splitting hyperplane.

SL2. [Grow tree taller.] If LN is the root, create a new root whose only entry is $(q_{LN}, \mathbf{E^d}, CP)$. Here, CP is a convex polyhedron with at most k faces that encloses all cells in the cell tree, and q_{LN} is a pointer to LN.

SL3. [Create subleaves.] LN_1 and LN_2 are empty leaves initially. For each entry $E_i(LN)$, test if the cell $E_i(LN).Z$ overlaps the halfspace H_r $(r=1,2)$. If yes, add a new entry E to LN_r, where $E.Z=E_i(LN).Z \cap H_r$ and $E.D=E_i(LN).D$.

SL4. [Create new entries.] Let q_1 and q_2 be pointers to LN_1 and LN_2, respectively. Create two new entries $E_{LN_r}=(q_r, E_{LN}.P \cap H_r, E_{LN}.C \cap H_r)$ $(r=1,2)$ and replace E_{LN} by E_{LN_1} and E_{LN_2}.

SL5. [Propagate split upwards.] If LN's ancestor node N has now more than M entries, **SplitNode(***N***)**.

When splitting an interior node N, one needs to maintain the condition that the number of partitions on each side of the splitting hyperplane is at least m. Furthermore, the splitting hyperplane should intersect a minimal number of polyhedra $E_i(N).C$ because each such intersection has to be propagated down the tree. A large number of such intersections may cause the split to become very costly.

Note that the hyperplane $H^*(N)$ corresponding to the root node of N's BSP-tree does not intersect *any* of the polyhedra $E_i(N).P$ (or $E_i(N).C$). Therefore a split using $H^*(N)$ would not have to be propagated down the tree. For that reason, in the cell tree an interior node will *only* be split if the hyperplane $H^*(N)$ is suitable for splitting, i.e. if the number of partitions on both sides of $H^*(N)$ is at least m. If that is not the case, N will not be split. It will rather be stored using overflow pages. Whenever another entry is added to N, however, another attempt will be made to split N along the hyperplane $H^*(N)$.

Algorithm **SplitNode(N)**. Given an overloaded interior node N in a cell tree, split N along a hyperplane, and propagate the split up the tree if necessary.

SN1. [Find hyperplane.] Check if the number of partitions on both sides of $H^*(N)$ is at least m. If no, stop. Otherwise, let H_1 and H_2 denote the two disjoint halfspaces that are defined by the hyperplane $H^*(N)$.

SN2. [Grow tree taller.] If N is the root, create a new root whose only entry is $(q_N, \mathbf{E}^d, CP)$. Here, CP is a convex polyhedron with at most k faces that encloses all cells in the cell tree, and q_N is a pointer to N.

SN3. [Create subnodes.] N_1 and N_2 are empty nodes initially. For each entry $E_i(N)$, test if $E_i(N).P \subseteq H_r$ ($r=1,2$). If yes, add the entry $E_i(N)$ to N_r.

SN4. [Create new entries.] Let q_1 and q_2 be pointers to N_1 and N_2, respectively. Create two new entries $E_{N_r}=(q_r, E_N.P \cap H_r, E_N.C \cap H_r)$ ($r=1,2$) and replace E_N by E_{N_1} and E_{N_2}.

SN5. [Propagate split upwards.] If N's ancestor node A has now more than M entries, **SplitNode(A)**.

Due to the fact that the polyhedra $E_i(N).P$ are partitions of a BSP, step SN3 can be carried out very efficiently as follows. The hyperplane $H^*(N)$ corresponds to the root of N's BSP tree. The two BSP subtrees below that root correspond to BSP's of the polyhedra $E_N.P \cap H_1$ and $E_N.P \cap H_2$. Each partition in those BSP's is also a partition of the original BSP of $E_N.P$. Therefore, all that has to be done is to copy these BSP subtrees into the corresponding subnodes N_1 and N_2.

The probability that $H^*(N)$ is not suitable for splitting can be computed as follows. As above, let M denote the maximum number of entries that can be stored on one disk page. The total number of partitions in an overloaded node is at least $M+1$. Hence, after $H^*(N)$ was first established (viz., when $E_N.P$ was split for the first time), at least $M-1$ more partitions were formed by further splittings of $E_N.P$. Assuming that the cells in the subtree rooted at N are distributed equally across the subspace $E_N.P$, the probability that the number of partitions on any side of $H^*(N)$ is less than m is

$$0.5^{M-1} \cdot \left[1 + \binom{M-1}{1} + \binom{M-1}{2} + \ldots + \binom{M-1}{m-2} \right]$$

As this probability depends on M, it is important to keep m reasonably low. For $m=3$ and $M=28$, for example, we obtain a probability of less than one in a million.

5.5.4. Tree Condensation

The tree condensation eliminates empty leaves and propagates the elimination up the tree. Interior nodes with less than m entries are deleted and the entries under these nodes are reinserted into the cell tree.

Algorithm **CondenseTree**(LN). Given an empty leaf node LN, eliminate LN and propagate the elimination up the tree.

CT1. [Initialize.] Set $N=LN$. Set Q, the set of eliminated leaf node entries, to be empty.

CT2. [Test for root.] If N is the root then go to CT5.

CT3. [Eliminate underloaded node.] If N has m or more entries, go to CT6. Otherwise, delete E_N from its ancestor node, add the leaf node entries under N to Q, and extend the polyhedra $E_{N_i}.P$ of N's siblings N_i to cover $E_N.P$.

CT4. [Move up one level in the tree.] Set N to its ancestor node and repeat from CT2.

CT5. [Shorten tree.] If the root N has only one entry then make N's only descendant node the new root.

CT6. [Reinsert orphaned leaf node entries.] For each entry E in Q, **InsertComponent**(T, $E.D$, $E.Z$), where T denotes the root of the cell tree.

The polyhedron extension in step CT3 can be carried out very efficiently as follows. Let N_i denote the siblings of node N. The polyhedra $E_{N_i}.P$ and $E_N.P$ are the partitions of a BSP and stored as a BSP-tree. Let LN_N be the BSP-tree leaf corresponding to the partition $E_N.P$. If LN_N's ancestor node is replaced by LN_N's sibling, the resulting tree represents a different BSP. This BSP is derived from the original BSP by deleting the partition $E_N.P$ and extending the partitions $E_{N_i}.P$ to cover $E_N.P$ (see fig. 5.7). This follows from the following lemma.

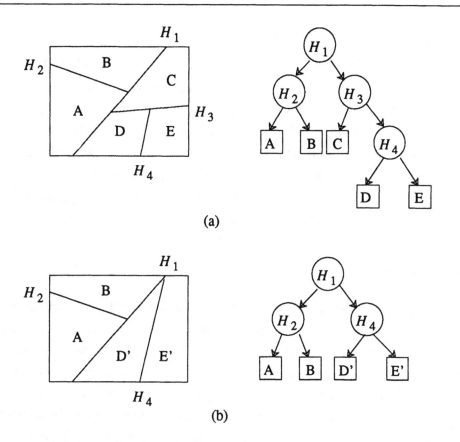

(a)

(b)

Figure 5.7: The BSP in (b) is obtained from the BSP in (a) by deleting the partition C and enlarging the partitions D and E such that they include C's area. In the BSP tree this corresponds to a substitution of C's ancestor node (H_3) by its sibling node (H_4).

Lemma 5.1: Let **P** denote some BSP, and let *LN* denote some leaf node in the BSP-tree corresponding to **P**. If *LN*'s ancestor is replaced by *LN*'s sibling, the BSP **P'** that corresponds to the resulting BSP-tree has the following properties:

(i)   **P'** has one partition less than **P**.

(ii)   Each partition in **P'** is a superset of some partition in **P**.

(iii) Each partition in **P** other than the one corresponding to *LN* is a subset of some partition in **P'**.

Proof:

(i) The tree transformation decreases the number of leaves by one. Hence, the number of partitions in the corresponding BSP decreases by one as well.

(ii) The tree transformation decreases the number of interior nodes by one. This corresponds to the removal of one of one of the hyperplanes defining the BSP. Hence, the partitions in $\mathbf{P}'$ are either identical to some partition in $\mathbf{P}$, or they are derived from some partition in $\mathbf{P}$ by removing one of the defining hyperplanes. In any case, they are a superset of some partition in $\mathbf{P}$.

(iii) The tree transformation deletes the leaf corresponding to partition $E_{LN}.P$. This, together with (i) and (ii), implies (iii). □

5.6. Summary

We presented the design of a database index for multidimensional geometric data, termed cell tree. All data objects in the database are represented as convex chains. The cell tree indexes the set of cells by means of a binary space partitioning. It is a fully dynamic data structure, i.e. insertions and deletions may be interleaved with searches and no periodic reorganization is required. Moreover, the cell tree is designed for paged memory; it represents an attempt to minimize the number of page faults per search operation. Each tree node corresponds to a disk page, and no pages other than those containing the cell tree will be required to answer a given search query. This is an important advantage of the cell tree over the R-tree and related structures, where data objects may have to be retrieved from memory, thereby causing additional page faults.

Compared to related data structures such as the R-tree, we believe that the cell tree is particularly efficient for point queries and for data objects that are not intervals (boxes) themselves. We are currently working on the implementation of the cell tree and are testing various sets of parameters.

Chapter 6

The Arc Tree: An Approximation Scheme
To Represent Arbitrary Curved Shapes

6.1. Introduction

The exact representation of curved geometric objects in finite machines is only possible if the objects can be described by finite mathematical expressions. Typical examples for such objects are paraboloids or ellipses, which can be described by functional equations such as $x^2/a^2+y^2/b^2=1$. Many applications, however, especially in computer vision and robotics, do not fit this pattern. The objects to be represented are rather arbitrary in shape, and some approximation scheme has to be employed to represent the data. Any finite machine can only store an approximate representation of the data with limited accuracy. In particular, the answer to any query is based on this approximate representation and may therefore be approximate as well.

Of course, the initial description of a curved object, coming from a camera, a tactile sensor, a mouse, or a digitizer may already be an *approximate* description of the real object. In most practical applications, this description will be a sequence of curve points or a spline, i.e. a piecewise polynomial function that is smooth and continuous. To support set, search, and recognition operators, however, it is more efficient to represent the data by a *hierarchy of detail* [Same84, Hopc87], i.e. a hierarchy of approximations, where higher levels in the hierarchy correspond to coarser approximations of the curve. Geometric operators can then be computed in a hierarchical manner: algorithms start out near the root of the hierarchy and try to answer the given query at a very coarse resolution. If that is not possible, the resolution is increased where necessary. In other words, algorithms "zoom in" on those parts of the curve that are relevant for the given query.

In this chapter, we develop this theme of hierarchy of detail, focusing on the *arc tree*, a balanced binary tree that serves as an approximation scheme to represent arbitrary curved shapes. Section 6.2 gives a definition of the arc tree and shows how to obtain the arc tree representation of a given curve. Section 6.3 generalizes the concept of the arc tree to include other hierarchical curve representation schemes such as Ballard's strip trees [Ball81] and Bezier curves [Bezi74, Pavl82]. Sections 6.4 and 6.5 show how to perform point queries and set operations, such as union or intersection. Both sections also discuss the performance of our arc tree implementation. Section 6.6 outlines how to embed arc trees into an extensible database system such as POSTGRES [Ston86a], and section 6.7 contains a summary and our conclusions.

6.2. Definition

A *curve* is a one-dimensional continuous point set in d-dimensional Euclidean space E^d. For simplicity, this presentation is restricted to the case $d=2$. The generalization to arbitrary d (with the curve remaining one-dimensional) is straightforward. A curve is *open* if it has two distinct endpoints, otherwise it is called *closed*; see figure 6.1 for some examples. As mentioned in the introduction, in practical applications, curves are usually given as a polygonal path, i.e. a sequence of curve points, or as a spline, i.e. a piecewise polynomial function that is smooth and continuous.

Figure 6.1: A closed and two open curves.

The arc tree scheme parametrizes a given curve according to its arc length and approximates it by a sequence of polygonal paths. Let the curve C have length l and be defined by a function $C(t):[0,1]\rightarrow E^2$, such that the length of the curve from $C(0)$ to $C(t_0)$ is $t_0 \cdot l$. The k-th approximation C_k $(k=0,1,2...)$ of C is a polygonal path consisting of 2^k line segments $e_{k,i}$ $(i=1..2^k)$, such that $e_{k,i}$ connects the two points $C(\frac{i-1}{2^k})$ and $C(\frac{i}{2^k})$. See figure 6.2 for an example.

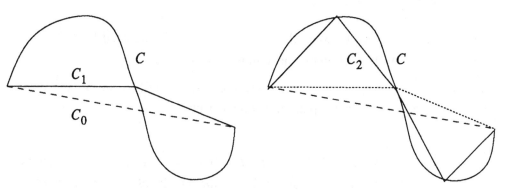

Figure 6.2: A 0th, 1st and 2nd approximation of a curve

Each edge $e_{k,i}$ can be associated with an arc $a_{k,i}$ of length $l/2^k$, which is a continuous subset of C. $C(\frac{i-1}{2^k})$ and $C(\frac{i}{2^k})$ are the common endpoints of $e_{k,i}$ and $a_{k,i}$. For $k \geq 1$, each k-th approximation is a refinement of the corresponding $(k-1)$-th approximation: the vertex set of the $(k-1)$-th approximation is a true subset of the vertex set of the k-th approximation.

More formally, the k-th approximation of C is defined by a piecewise linear function $C_k(t):[0,1] \rightarrow E^2$ as follows. Here, $\underline{t}$ and $\overline{t}$ denote $\dfrac{\left\lfloor t \cdot 2^k \right\rfloor}{2^k}$ and $\dfrac{\left\lceil t \cdot 2^k \right\rceil}{2^k}$, respectively.

$$C_k(t) = \begin{cases} C(t) & t \cdot 2^k = 0..2^k \\ \dfrac{\overline{t}-t}{\overline{t}-\underline{t}} \cdot C(\underline{t}) + \dfrac{t-\underline{t}}{\overline{t}-\underline{t}} \cdot C(\overline{t}) & \text{otherwise} \end{cases}$$

There are various criteria in common use that measure the error between a curve C and its k-th polygonal approximation C_k [Imai86]. In the case of the arc tree, one could use the maximum distance between a curve point and the corresponding point of the approximation:

$$\max_{0 \leq t \leq 1} d(C_k(t), C(t))$$

Here, d denotes Euclidean distance. This criterion will be referred to as (e1). Other possibilities include the maximum distance between a line segment $e_{k,i}$ and the curve points on the corresponding arc $a_{k,i}$ (e2):

$$\max_{0\le t\le 1} d(e_{k,\left\lceil t\cdot 2^k\right\rceil},C(t))$$

or the maximum distance between the *line* containing $e_{k,i}$ (denoted by $line(e_{k,i})$) and the arc $a_{k,i}$ (e3). The following theorem is easily proven.

Theorem 6.1: According to any of the error criteria described above, the error between a curve C and its k-th approximation C_k is no more than $l/2^{k+1}$.

Proof:

(e1) For some arbitrary but fixed t ($0\le t\le 1$) consider the triangle $\Delta(C(\underline{t}),C(t),C(\overline{t}))$. Let a, b and c denote the lengths of its edges as marked in figure 6.3. Also, let r denote the distance ratio $\dfrac{d(C(\underline{t}),C_k(t))}{d(C(\underline{t}),C(\overline{t}))}$ ($0\le r\le 1$). As the length of the arc between $C(\underline{t})$ and $C(\overline{t})$ is $l/2^k$, we obtain

$$b \le \frac{r\cdot l}{2^k} \quad \text{and}$$

$$a \le \frac{(1-r)\cdot l}{2^k}$$

On the other hand, with some trigonometry we obtain for the distance x between the curve point $C(t)$ and its corresponding approximation point $C_k(t)$

$$x^2 = b^2 + r^2c^2 - rb^2 - rc^2 + ra^2$$

$$\le (1-r)\cdot b^2 + ra^2$$

$$\le \frac{(1-r)\cdot r^2\cdot l^2}{2^{2k}} + \frac{r\cdot(1-r)^2\cdot l^2}{2^{2k}}$$

$$= (r-r^2)\cdot\frac{l^2}{2^{2k}}$$

This expression is maximal for $r=1/2$. Therefore

$$x^2 \le \frac{l^2}{4\cdot 2^{2k}} \quad \text{or}$$

$$d(C(t),C_k(t)) \le l/2^{k+1}$$

which proves the theorem for this case.

(e2) Suppose there were a t ($0\le t\le 1$) such that

$$d(e_{k,\left\lceil t\cdot 2^k\right\rceil},C(t)) > l/2^{k+1}.$$

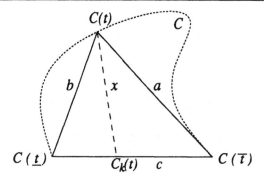

Figure 6.3: $\Delta(C(\underline{t}),C(t),C(\overline{t}))$ with a subcurve of curve C.

Then we have

$$d(C_k(\underline{t}),C(t)) + d(C(t),C_k(\overline{t})) > 2 \cdot 1/2^{k+1} \quad \text{or}$$

$$d(C(\underline{t}),C(t)) + d(C(t),C(\overline{t})) > 1/2^k$$

This is a contradiction to the definition of the k-th approximation. The arc from $C(\underline{t})$ to $C(\overline{t})$ may not be longer than $1/2^k$.

(e3) Suppose there were a t ($0 \leq t \leq 1$) such that

$$d(line\ (e_{k,\lceil t \cdot 2^k \rceil}),C(t)) > 1/2^{k+1}.$$

Then we have

$$d(C_k(\underline{t}),C(t)) + d(C(t),C_k(\overline{t})) > 2 \cdot 1/2^{k+1}$$

and contradiction as above. □

Lemma 6.2: Using any of the above error criteria, the sequence of approximation functions $(C_k(t))$ converges uniformly towards $C(t)$.

Proof: It follows from theorem 6.1 that the error converges towards zero for $k \to \infty$, which proves the lemma. □

Moreover, for each approximation C_k there is a well-defined area that contains the curve. We have

Lemma 6.3: Let $E_{k,i}$ denote the ellipse whose major axis is $1/2^k$ and whose focal points are the two endpoints of the edge $e_{k,i}$, $C(\frac{i-1}{2^k})$ and $C(\frac{i}{2^k})$. Then the arc

$a_{k,i}$ is internal to $E_{k,i}$.

Proof: (by contradiction) Let $X \in a_{k,i}$ denote a point external to $E_{k,i}$. Then

$$d(X, C(\frac{i-1}{2^k})) + d(X, C(\frac{i}{2^k})) > l/2^k$$

Thus, the length of $a_{k,i}$ would be greater than $l/2^k$ which is a contradiction. $\quad\square$

Corollary 6.4: The curve C is internal to the area formed by the union of the bounding ellipses, $\bigcup\limits_{i=0}^{2^k} E_{k,i}$ $(k=0, 1, ..)$. $\quad\square$

See figure 6.4 for an example.

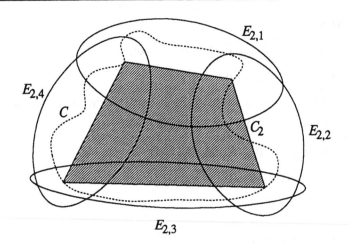

Figure 6.4: A curve C with its 2nd approximation C_2 and corresponding ellipses $E_{2,i}$.

The family of approximations of a given curve C can be stored efficiently in a binary tree. The root of the tree contains the three points $C(0)$, $C(1/2)$ and $C(1)$ and is considered on level 0. If a tree node on level i contains point $C(\frac{x}{2^{i+1}})$ $(x=1 .. 2^{i+1}-1)$, then its left son contains point $C(\frac{2x-1}{2^{i+2}})$, and its right son contains point $C(\frac{2x+1}{2^{i+2}})$. We call this tree the *arc tree* of the curve C. The arc tree is an exact representation of C; each of its subtrees represents a continous subset of C. An inorder traversal of the first k $(k \geq 0)$ levels of the arc tree yields the vertices of the $(k+1)$-th approximation, sorted by increasing t. On the other hand, a breadth-first traversal of the first k levels yields these vertices in an order such that the first 2^i+1 vertices yielded form the i-th approximation of C ($i=1,2 .. k+1$). See figure 6.5 for an example.

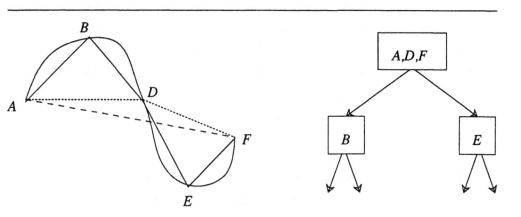

Figure 6.5: A curve with approximations and its arc tree. For a closed curve, it is $A = F$.

In practice, only a finite number of levels of the arc tree is stored. An arc tree with r levels is called an arc tree of *resolution* r. It is a balanced binary tree and it represents the 0th through $(r+1)$-th approximation of C.

An arc tree of resolution r can be constructed in two traversals of the given curve C. In the first round, one determines the length l of C. If C is a spline (or a polygonal path), l can be computed using the following formula for the arc length of an analytical curve. If the curve is given by $y = f(x)$, its length between the points $P_1(x_1,y_1)$ and $P_2(x_2,y_2)$ is

$$l = \int_{x_1}^{x_2} \sqrt{1+f'^2(x)}\,dx$$

If it is given by $x = x(t), y = y(t)$, its arc length is

$$l = \int_{t_1}^{t_2} \sqrt{x'^2(t)+y'^2(t)}\,dt$$

with $x_i = x(t_i)$ and $y_i = y(t_i)$. One may also attach a label to each knot of C indicating the length accumulated so far. This does not require any additional computation, but it will speed up the second round. In the second round, one picks up the curve points $C(\dfrac{i}{2^r})$ ($i \in \{0,1..2^r\}$) and inserts them into the appropriate tree nodes while performing an inorder traversal of the tree.

Note that arc trees can be used to represent any given curve that can be parametrized with respect to arc length. This requirement poses no problem if the input curve is given as a polygonal path or a spline. Nevertheless, there remain problems with some curves such as fractals, for example [Mand77], or with curves that are distorted by high-frequency noise. In both cases the concept of arc length becomes somewhat meaningless and it is necessary to smooth the curve first before the parametrization can take place.

6.3. Generalization

The arc tree parametrizes the given curve by arc length and localizes it by means of bounding ellipses. At higher resolutions the number of ellipses increases, but their total area decreases, thus providing a better localization.

The arc tree can be viewed as just one instance of a large class of approximation schemes that implement a hierarchy of detail. Higher levels in the hierarchy correspond to coarser approximations of the curve. Associated with each approximation is a *bounding area* that contains the curve. Set and search operators are computed in a hierarchical manner: algorithms start out near the root of the hierarchy and try to solve the given problem at a very coarse resolution. If that is not possible, the resolution is increased where necessary.

In this section we will present several approximation schemes that are based on the same principle, but that use different parametrizations or bounding areas. For all of these schemes, it is fairly straightforward to obtain the representation of a given curve. Moreover, the algorithms for the computation of set and search operators are very similar to the corresponding arc tree algorithms, which are presented in sections 6.4 and 6.5. It is a subject of further research to conduct a detailed practical comparison of these schemes to find out which schemes are suited best for certain classes of curves.

The first modification of the arc tree concerns the choice of the ellipses $E_{k,i}$ as bounding areas. These ellipses provide the tightest possible bound but, on the other hand, ellipses are fairly complex objects, which has a negative impact on the performance of this scheme. For example, it is often necessary to test two bounding areas for intersection; if the bounding areas are ellipses, this operation is rather costly. Our implementation showed that it is in fact sometimes more efficient to replace the ellipses by their bounding circles; see section 6.5.1. The circles provide a poorer localization of the curve, but they are easier to handle computationally, which caused the total performance to improve. Other alternatives would be to use bounding boxes whose axes are parallel to the coordinate axes or to the axes of the ellipses. Both of these approaches, however, proved to be less effective than the bounding circles.

If the curves to be represented are polygonal paths with relatively few vertices, it is more efficient to break up the polygonal paths at their vertices rather than to introduce artificial vertices $C(\frac{i}{2^k})$ $(i=1 .. 2^k-1)$. If a polygonal path has $n+1$ vertices $v_1 .. v_{n+1}$, it can be represented *exactly* by a *polygon arc tree* of depth $\lceil \log_2 n \rceil$ as follows. The root of the polygon arc tree contains the vertices v_1, $v_{\lceil n/2 \rceil +1}$, and v_{n+1}. Its left son contains the vertex $v_{\lceil n/4 \rceil +1}$, its right son the vertex $v_{\lceil 3/4 \cdot n \rceil +1}$, and so on, until all vertices are stored. Clearly, the arc length corresponding to a node is no more implicit; it has to be stored explicitly with each node. In particular, at each node N it is necessary to know the lengths of the subcurves corresponding to N's left and right subtree. An example is given in figure 6.6.

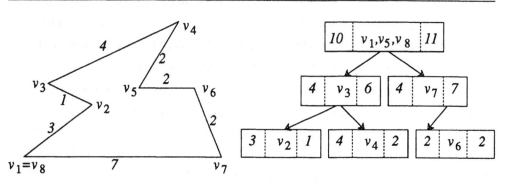

Figure 6.6: A polygon and corresponding polygon arc tree. The numbers in italics denote arc length.

It is easily seen that some of this length data is redundant. Indeed, with some care it is sufficient to store only one arc length datum per node. For this reason, the storage requirements for a polygon arc tree are only about 20% to 40% higher than for a regular arc tree of the same depth.

A data structure closely related to the polygon arc tree is the *Binary Searchable Polygonal Representation (BSPR)* proposed by Burton [Burt77].

There are other structures that also implement some hierarchy of detail. One of them is the *strip tree*, introduced by Ballard [Ball81]. As the arc tree, the strip tree represents a given curve C by a binary tree such that each subtree T represents a continuous part C_T of C. C_T is approximated by the line segment connecting its endpoints (x_b, y_b) and (x_e, y_e). The root node of T stores these two endpoints and two widths w_l and w_r, thus defining a bounding rectangle S_T (the *strip*) that tightly encloses the curve segment C_T. S_T has the same length as the line segment $((x_b, y_b), (x_e, y_e))$ and its sides are parallel or perpendicular to it. See figure 6.7 for an example of a curve and a corresponding strip tree. Clearly, this approach requires some extensions for closed curves and for curves that extend beyond their endpoints (fig. 6.8).

When a strip tree is constructed for a given curve C, a curve segment C_T is subdivided further until the total strip width $w_l + w_r$ is below a certain threshold. As it is a non-trivial operation to obtain the strip S_T for every curve segment C_T, the construction of a strip tree for a given curve may be quite costly. To subdivide C_T, one can choose any point of C_T that lies on the boundary of the corresponding strip S_T. Clearly, a strip tree is not necessarily balanced, which has a negative impact on its average-case performance. Note that arc trees are always balanced, which might give them an edge over strip trees in terms of average performance.

Also, a strip tree requires about twice as much space as an arc tree of same depth: each arc tree node stores a minimum of two real numbers and two pointers, whereas a strip tree node stores six real numbers and two pointers. Note, however, that strip trees can be modified to require less storage. First, all subdivision points belong to more than one strip and are therefore stored in more than one node. The redundant data may be replaced by pointers or deleted; in the latter case, the strip tree algorithms given by Ballard would have to be somewhat modified. Second, rather than storing w_l and w_r, one may just store the maximum of these two widths. The corresponding strip is potentially wider and provides a poorer localization. In both cases, some loss in performance is likely, but it will probably be minor compared to the savings in storage space.

A generalization of the strip tree to higher dimensions is possible. The *prism tree* of Ponce and Faugeras, for example [Ponc87], approximates free-form solids in

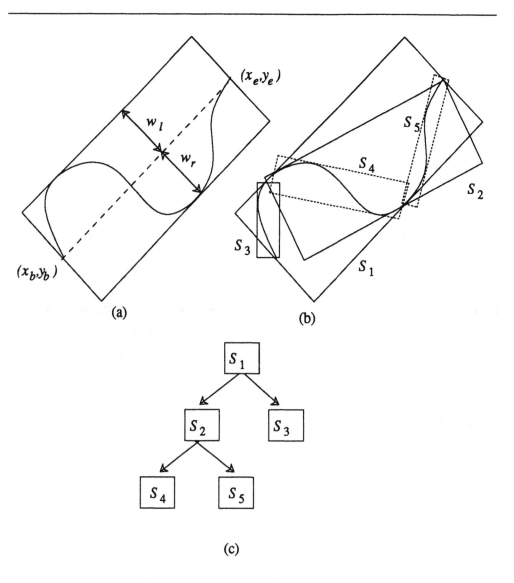

Figure 6.7: A curve with strip, a hierarchy of strips, and a corresponding strip tree.

three dimensions by means of truncated pyramids. The arc tree, on the other hand, does not have an immediate equivalent in higher dimensions because the parametrization method (by arc length) is impractical to generalize.

A very different approach to implement a hierarchy of detail is based on curve fitting techniques such as *Bezier curves* [Bezi74] or *B-splines* [Debo78]; see also

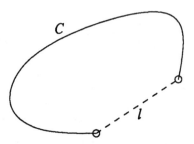

Figure 6.8: A curve C that extends beyond its endpoints. There is no bounding box of length l that contains C.

[Pavl82] for a good survey of these and related techniques. A Bezier curve of degree m is an m-th degree polynomial function defined by $m+1$ *guiding points* $P_1 .. P_{m+1}$. The curve goes through the points P_1 and P_{m+1} and passes near the remaining guiding points $P_2 .. P_m$ in a well-defined manner. The points P_2 through P_m may be relocated interactively to bring the Bezier curve into the desired form. See figure 6.9 for two examples.

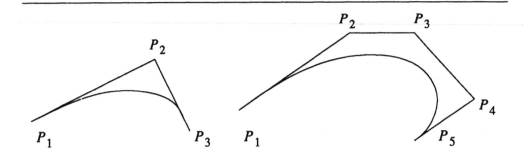

Figure 6.9: Examples of Bezier polynomials with three and five guiding points.

It can be shown that a Bezier curve lies within the corresponding *characteristic polygon*, i.e. the convex hull of its guiding points. Also, a Bezier curve B can be subdivided into two Bezier curves B_1 and B_2 of same degree. The characteristic polygons of B_1 and B_2 are disjoint and subsets of B's characteristic polygon. They therefore provide a better localization of B; see figure 6.10.

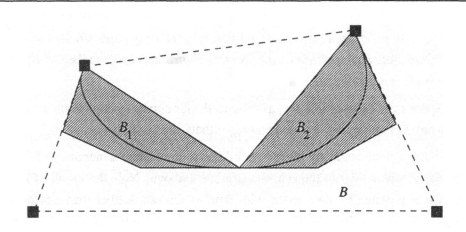

Figure 6.10: A Bezier curve B subdivided into two curves B_1 and B_2 with characteristic polygons.

Now we can derive a hierarchical representation of a given Bezier curve B as follows. The first approximation is the edge segment connecting B's endpoints; its bounding area is given by B's characteristic polygon. The second approximation is the polygonal path connecting the endpoints of B_1 and B_2; its bounding area is the union of the characteristic polygons of B_1 and B_2, and so on. There are various efficient subdivision algorithms to obtain B_1 and B_2 from a given B; see for example [Pavl82], pp. 221-230.

The main problem with this approach seems to be that not every curve can be approximated well by a low-order Bezier curve. A high-order Bezier curve, however, is harder to subdivide and has a more complex characteristic polygon, which has an adverse impact on the performance of this scheme. In practice, complex curves are often approximated by *several* third-order Bezier curves. This would mean that the bounding area of the first approximation is a union of convex polygons, which is already rather complex. Further approximations are then obtained by subdivisions of each one of these polygons. Nevertheless, this approach seems very promising and should be included in a practical comparison of the various approaches to implement a hierarchy of detail.

We expect arc or strip trees to be superior to Bezier curves if the curves to be represented are initially described by a long sequence of curve points and can only be described by high-order splines or a large number of simpler splines. This is often the case if curves are input from a digitizer pad or a mouse. On the other hand, if a curve is initially given by a few simple splines, it is probably more efficient to keep this representation and use spline subdivision algorithms as described above to implement a hierarchy of detail.

B-splines can be used in a way similar to Bezier curves to implement a hierarchy of detail. For appropriate subdivision algorithms, see [Bohm84].

Certainly, there are many more possibilities to implement a hierarchy of detail as a tree structure similar to the schemes presented above. Note that in all of these schemes it is possible to trade space with time as follows. Rather than storing all lower level approximations explicitly, one could keep the source description of the curve in main memory and compute finer approximations "on the fly" when needed. This approach can be viewed as a *procedural arc tree* as finer approximations are defined procedurally, i.e. by means of the appropriate subdivision algorithm that computes finer approximations from coarser ones. This approach seems particularly promising for the Bezier approach where highly efficient subdivision algorithms are available. In the case of arc and strip trees, the computations to obtain finer approximations are probably too complex to be repeated at every tree traversal.

As mentioned above, the algorithms for set and search operations for these various approximation schemes are all essentially the same. In the following two sections, we give the algorithms for the arc tree scheme. In most cases, the corresponding algorithms for the other schemes are simply obtained by replacing the ellipses $E_{k,i}$ by the corresponding bounding areas, viz., the characteristic polygons for the curve fitting approaches or the strips for the strip tree.

6.4. Hierarchical Point Inclusion Test

To demonstrate the power of the arc tree representation scheme, we first show how to answer point queries on the arc tree. Given a point $A \in E^2$ and a simple (i.e. non self-intersecting) closed curve C, a point query asks if A is internal to the point set enclosed by C, $P(C)$. For simplicity, we also describe this case by stating that A is internal to C, or that $A \in P(C)$.

The point inclusion test is performed by a hierarchical algorithm called *HPOINT*, which starts with some simple approximation C_{app} of C. For each edge $e_{k,i}$ of C_{app} ($i=1..2^k$), it checks if the replacement of $e_{k,i}$ by the arc $a_{k,i}$ may affect the internal/external classification of A. If there is no such edge $e_{k,i}$, then $A \in P(C_{app})$ is equivalent to $A \in P(C)$; *HPOINT* uses a conventional algorithm for polygons to solve the point query $A \in P(C_{app})$? and terminates with that result. Otherwise, *HPOINT* replaces each edge $e_{k,i}$, whose replacement by $a_{k,i}$ may affect A's classification, by the two edges $e_{k+1,2i-1}$ and $e_{k+1,2i}$. *HPOINT* proceeds with the resulting polygon, which is a closer approximation of C.

If the maximum resolution has been reached without obtaining a result, then the problem cannot be decided at that resolution. In fact, there are boundary points (such as $C(1/3)$) that cannot be decided at *any* finite resolution. There are three ways to resolve this situation: (i) the algorithm returns *unclear*, (ii) the algorithm considers the point a boundary point, or (iii) the arc tree is extended at its leaf nodes to include the source description of the curve; then, edges $e_{k,i}$ may eventually be replaced by arcs $a_{k,i}$ to allow an exact query evaluation. For *HPOINT*, we choose option (ii), thus considering the boundary as having a nonzero width. In our definition of the point inclusion test, where the given point set $P(C)$ is closed, *HPOINT* returns $A \in P(C)$, accordingly.

We are left with the problem of how to find out quickly if the replacement of $e_{k,i}$ by $a_{k,i}$ may affect the internal/external classification of A. From lemma 6.3, we obtain

Lemma 6.5: Let $C_{k,i}$ denote the curve obtained from C by replacing the arc $a_{k,i}$ by the straight line $e_{k,i}$. If A is external to $E_{k,i}$ then $A \in P(C)$ is equivalent to $A \in P(C_{k,i})$.

Proof: Because A is external to $E_{k,i}$, A may not lie on or between $a_{k,i}$ and $e_{k,i}$. Therefore, the replacement of $a_{k,i}$ by $e_{k,i}$ may not affect the internal/external classification of A. □

It is therefore sufficient to check if A is internal to $E_{k,i}$. If yes, the replacement of $e_{k,i}$ by $a_{k,i}$ may affect the classification of A, otherwise it may not. Letting the initial approximation be C_0, *HPOINT* can be described more precisely as follows.

Algorithm HPOINT

Input: A point $A \in \mathbf{E}^2$. The arc tree T_C of a simple closed curve C.

Output: $A \in P(C)$?

(1)   Set the approximation polygon C_{app} to C_0, k to zero, and tag the edge $e_{0,1}$ of C_{app}.

(2)   For each tagged edge $e_{k,i}$ ($i \in \{1..2^k\}$) of C_{app}, check if A is external to the ellipse $E_{k,i}$. If yes, untag $e_{k,i}$.

(3)   If C_{app} has no tagged edges left, use a conventional point inclusion algorithm for polygons to determine if $A \in P(C_{app})$, return the result and stop.

(4)   Otherwise, if k is less than the maximum resolution, *depth* (T_C), replace each tagged edge $e_{k,i}$ by the two tagged edges $e_{k+1,2i-1}$ and $e_{k+1,2i}$, increase k by one and repeat from (2).

(5)   Otherwise, A is a boundary point; return *true* and stop.

Step (2) can easily be done by computing the distances from A to the two focal points of $E_{k,i}$. Step (4) can be performed by using C's arc tree in the following manner. Each edge $e_{k,i}$ is associated with the subtree whose root contains the point $C(\frac{2i-1}{2^{k+1}})$. Note that this is the curve point which corresponds to the center point of $e_{k,i}$ and which $e_{k+1,2i-1}$ and $e_{k+1,2i}$ have in common. If $e_{k,i}$ is to be replaced by $e_{k+1,2i-1}$ and $e_{k+1,2i}$, *HPOINT* obtains that point from the tree node and continues recursively on both subtrees of this node.

Steps (2) and (4) can now be performed during a top-down traversal of the arc tree. Each subtree can be processed independently of the others, which offers a natural way to parallelize the algorithm. If C_{app} has no more tagged edges, then the partial results are collected in a bottom-up traversal of the tree and put together to form the boundary of the final approximation polygon C_{app}. At this point, $A \in P(C)$ is equivalent to $A \in P(C_{app})$. Step (4) can be performed by Shamos' algorithm, where one constructs a horizontal line L through A and counts the intersections between L and the edges of C_{app} that lie to the left of A. If the number of intersections is odd, then A is internal, otherwise it is external. Shamos' algorithm requires some special maintenance for horizontal edges; see [Prep85] for details.

We implemented this algorithm on a VAX 8800 and ran several experiments to see how *HPOINT*'s time complexity correlates with the complexity of the given curve C and with the location of A with respect to C. Our running times should not be considered in absolute terms as we did not make a great effort to optimize our code. However, the figures are appropriate for comparative measurements. Figures 6.11 and 6.12 show our results. Here, t is CPU time in ms, and r is the resolution at which the query was decided. The dotted polygons are the final approximations C_{app}, respectively.

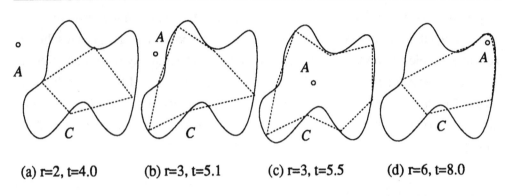

| (a) r=2, t=4.0 | (b) r=3, t=5.1 | (c) r=3, t=5.5 | (d) r=6, t=8.0 |

Figure 6.11: C is a spline with 12 knots.

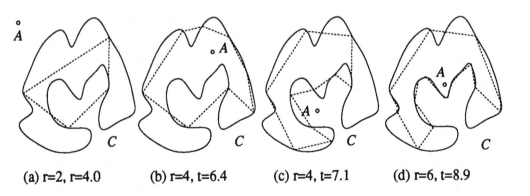

| (a) r=2, r=4.0 | (b) r=4, t=6.4 | (c) r=4, t=7.1 | (d) r=6, t=8.9 |

Figure 6.12: C is a spline with 36 knots.

Note that the use of alternative approximation schemes is unlikely to improve the performance of our algorithms. To test a given point for inclusion in a given ellipse has about the same complexity as the corresponding tests for a characteristic polygon (say, a convex quadrilateral) or a strip. On the other hand, the test is somewhat easier for circles or for boxes whose axes are parallel to the coordinate axes. In both cases, however, the localization of the curve that is provided by these areas is poorer than for the bounding areas above.

Our algorithm *HPOINT* is an application of the idea of *hierarchy of detail*, as described by Samet [Same84] or Hopcroft and Krafft [Hopc87]. It solves the point inclusion problem by starting with a very simple representation of C and introduces more complex representations only if they are required to solve the problem. The algorithm "zooms in" on those parts of C that are interesting in the sense that they may change the internal/external classification of the point A at a higher resolution. As our examples demonstrate, *HPOINT* terminates very quickly if A is not close to C. The closer A gets to C, the higher is the resolution required to answer the point query. Due to a quick localization of the interesting parts of C, the algorithm does not show the quadratic growth in the complexity of C that a worst-case analysis would predict.

6.5. Hierarchical Set Operations

In this section, we show how to detect and compute intersections, unions, and differences of one- and two-dimensional point sets. We assume that the input point sets are simple (i.e. no self-intersections or holes) and that they are given by their arc trees or by the arc trees of their boundaries. Again, the idea is to inspect approximations of the input curves by increasing resolution and to "zoom in" on those parts of the boundaries that may participate in an intersection.

6.5.1. Curve-Curve Intersection Detection

We first show how to test two given curves C and D for intersection. The hierarchical algorithm *HCURVES* starts with simple approximations C_{app} and D_{app} of C and D, respectively, and continues with approximations of higher resolutions where necessary. We have

Lemma 6.6: The arcs $a_{k,i}$ and $b_{k,j}$ corresponding to the edges $e_{k,i}$ of C_{app} and $f_{k,j}$ of D_{app}, respectively, *must* intersect if the following three conditions are met:

(i) $e_{k,i}$ intersects $f_{k,j}$,

(ii)   the two endpoints of $e_{k,i}$ are external to the ellipse $F_{k,j}$ corresponding to $f_{k,j}$,

(iii)   the two endpoints of $f_{k,j}$ are external to the ellipse $E_{k,i}$ corresponding to $e_{k,i}$.

Proof: Any situation where all three conditions are met are topologically equivalent to the situation in figure 6.13.

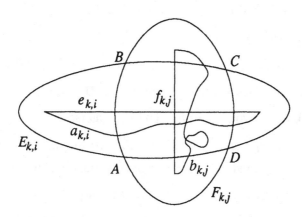

Figure 6.13: The arcs $a_{k,i}$ and $b_{k,j}$ *must* intersect.

The intersection of the two ellipses $E_{k,i}$ and $F_{k,j}$ is a quadrilateral ABCD with curved edges AB, BC, CD, and DA. The segment of the arc $a_{k,i}$ that is interior to ABCD connects some point of AB with some point of CD. The segment of the arc $b_{k,i}$ that is interior to ABCD connects some point of BC with some point of DA. Obviously, this is not possible without an intersection of the two arc segments, which proves the lemma.   □

Now the algorithm *HCURVES* proceeds as follows. For each pair of edges, $e_{k,i}$ of C_{app} and $f_{k,j}$ of D_{app} $(i,j \in \{0,1..2^k\})$, *HCURVES* checks if their corresponding arcs *may* intersect. According to lemma 6.3, this can be done by testing if the corresponding ellipses $E_{k,i}$ and $F_{k,j}$ intersect. If yes, *HCURVES* puts tags on $e_{k,i}$ and $f_{k,j}$ and applies lemma 6.6 to see if the arcs *must* intersect. If yes, *HCURVES* reports an intersection and stops. After all pairs of edges have been processed, *HCURVES* checks if there are any tagged edges. If no, *HCURVES* reports no intersection and stops. Otherwise, *HCURVES* replaces all tagged edges by the corresponding edges of the next higher approximation, increases k by one, and proceeds with the refined curves. If the maximum resolution has been reached and there are still tagged edges, *HCURVES* interprets the situation as an intersection of the boundaries and returns an intersection. More exactly, *HCURVES* can be described as follows.

Algorithm HCURVES

Input: The arc trees T_C and T_D of two curves C and D.

Output: $C \cap D \neq \emptyset$?

(1)　Set the approximation polygons C_{app} to C_0, D_{app} to D_0, and k to zero.

(2)　For each pair of edges $e_{k,i}$ of C_{app} and $f_{k,j}$ of D_{app} do

　　(2a)　Check if the two ellipses $E_{k,i}$ and $F_{k,j}$ intersect.

　　(2b)　If yes, tag $e_{k,i}$ and $f_{k,j}$; if conditions (i) through (iii) in lemma 6.6 are met or if $e_{k,i}$ and $f_{k,j}$ share one or two endpoints, return *true* and stop.

(3)　If there are no tagged edges, return *false* and stop.

(4)　If k is less than the maximum resolution, $\min(depth(T_C), depth(T_D))$, replace each tagged edge $e_{k,i}$ of C_{app} by the two edges $e_{k+1,2i-1}$ and $e_{k+1,2i}$. Similarly for each tagged edge $f_{k,j}$ of D_{app}. Increase k by one and repeat from (2).

(5)　Otherwise, the maximum resolution has been reached; return *true* and stop.

We implemented this algorithm on a VAX 8800 with a few slight modifications to speed up execution. First, the test if the two ellipses $E_{k,i}$ and $F_{k,j}$ intersect is replaced by a test if the two circumscribing circles of $E_{k,i}$ and $F_{k,j}$ intersect. If those do not intersect then the ellipses do not intersect either. Otherwise, we assume that the ellipses may intersect and proceed accordingly. We made several experiments with more accurate tests, such as to test bounding boxes of the two ellipses for intersection, or to test the two ellipses themselves for intersection. In every case, the execution times went up between 25% and 60%. The more accurate tests required a significant amount of CPU time, but they only marginally reduced the number of tagged edges.

Second, rather than performing step (2) for each pair of edges $e_{k,i}$ of C_{app} and $f_{k,j}$ of D_{app}, we maintain a list to keep track which pairs of ellipses $(E_{k,i}, F_{k,j})$ pass the intersection test in step (2a). Then, step (2) is executed for a pair of edges

$(e_{k,i}, f_{k,j})$ if and only if the ellipses $E_{k-1,\lceil i/2 \rceil}$ and $F_{k-1,\lceil j/2 \rceil}$, which correspond to their parent edges, intersect. Otherwise, it is known in advance that $E_{k,i}$ and $F_{k,j}$ do not intersect.

Figures 6.14 and 6.15 give several examples for the performance of the algorithm. Here, r denotes the resolution at which the algorithm is able to decide the query, and t denotes the CPU time in ms.

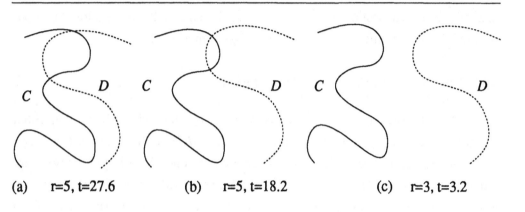

(a)   r=5, t=27.6   (b)   r=5, t=18.2   (c)   r=3, t=3.2

Figure 6.14: C is a spline with 13 knots, D a spline with 8 knots.

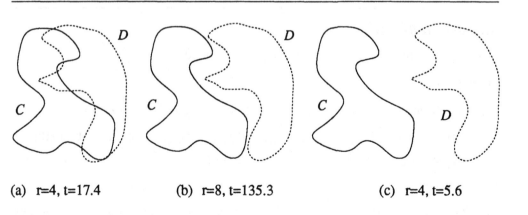

(a) r=4, t=17.4   (b) r=8, t=135.3   (c) r=4, t=5.6

Figure 6.15: C is a spline with 24 knots, D a spline with 23 knots.

Again, it is not clear if the use of alternative approximation schemes might yield a better performance. The crucial operation in algorithm *HCURVES* is the test if two bounding areas intersect. In the case of circles, this is a trivial operation: two circles intersect if the distance between their centers is no more than the sum of their radii. The corresponding tests for boxes or characteristic polygons (say, convex quadrilaterals) are about two to three times as complex.

Note that the running times do not grow quadratically with the complexity of the input curves. The example in figure 6.15 (b) requires a large amount of CPU time due to the fact that the two curves are quite interwoven but do not intersect. It is therefore necessary to get down to fairly high resolutions in order to determine that there is no intersection. It seems that a case like this will require a lot of computation with any other intersection detection algorithm as well.

6.5.2. Curve-Curve Intersection Computation

The intersection is actually computed by the hierarchical algorithm *HCRVCRV*, a variation of algorithm *HCURVES*. *HCRVCRV* does not test if two arcs *must* intersect. It continues the refinement until one of the following two conditions is met: (i) there are no more tagged edges, or (ii) the maximum resolution has been reached. In case (i), C and D do not intersect. In case (ii), each tagged edge of C_{app} is intersected with each tagged edge of D_{app} and the intersection points are returned.

Algorithm HCRVCRV

Input: The arc trees T_C and T_D of two curves C and D.

Output: $C \cap D$

(1) Set the approximation polygons C_{app} to C_0, D_{app} to D_0, and k to zero.

(2) For each pair of edges $e_{k,i}$ of C_{app} and $f_{k,j}$ of D_{app}, check if the two ellipses $E_{k,i}$ and $F_{k,j}$ intersect. If yes, tag $e_{k,i}$ and $f_{k,j}$.

(3) If there are no tagged edges, return *no intersection* and stop.

(4) Otherwise, if k is less than the maximum resolution, $min(depth\,(T_C),depth\,(T_D))$, replace each tagged edge $e_{k,i}$ of C_{app} by the two edges $e_{k+1,2i-1}$ and $e_{k+1,2i}$. Similarly for each tagged edge $f_{k,j}$ of D_{app}. Increase k by one and repeat from (2).

(5) Otherwise, the maximum resolution has been reached. Intersect each tagged edge $e_{k,i}$ with each tagged edge $f_{k,j}$, report all intersection points and stop.

We implemented this algorithm on a VAX 8800 with the same modifications as in the case of *HCURVES*. Figures 6.16 and 6.17 give two examples for the performance of the algorithm at various maximum resolutions r. P is an intersection point, d is the distance between P and its approximation, C_{app} and D_{app} are C's and D's final approximations, and t is CPU time required to compute all intersections.

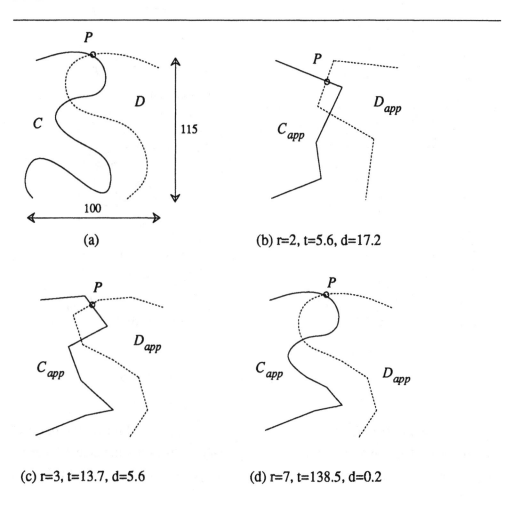

(a)

(b) r=2, t=5.6, d=17.2

(c) r=3, t=13.7, d=5.6

(d) r=7, t=138.5, d=0.2

Figure 6.16: C is a spline with 13 knots, D a spline with 8 knots.

Note that the running times do not increase quadratically with the number of edges, 2^r, or with the complexity of the input curves. In fact, the increase in CPU time is about cubical in r, i.e. polylogarithmic in the number of edges. The plot in

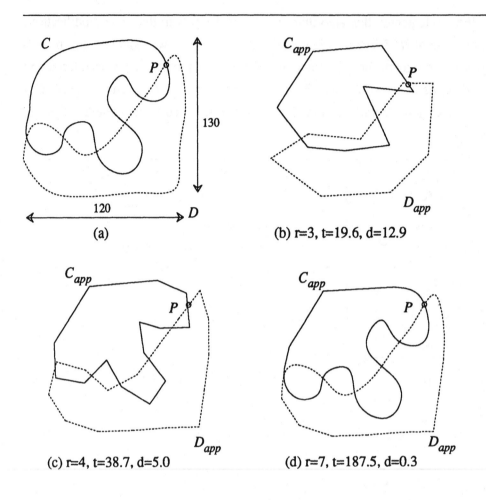

(a)

(b) r=3, t=19.6, d=12.9

(c) r=4, t=38.7, d=5.0

(d) r=7, t=187.5, d=0.3

Figure 6.17: Both C and D are splines with 20 knots.

figure 6.18 shows the increase in CPU time for both figures and for resolutions $r=2$ through $r=7$. The broken lines indicate the distance d between the actual intersection point P and the corresponding intersection point returned by $HCRVCRV$ at maximum resolution r.

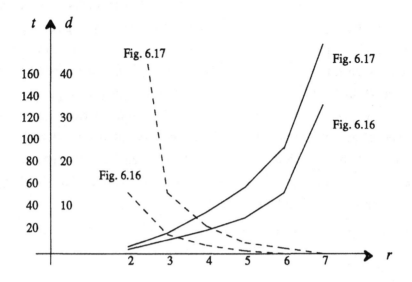

Figure 6.18: CPU time t and error d of algorithm *HCRVCRV* at various resolutions r.

6.5.3. Curve-Area Intersection Detection

Given the arc trees of a curve C and a closed curve D, it is now easy to detect if C intersects the point set $P(D)$. First, one employs algorithm *HCURVES* to check C and D for intersection. If the two curves do not intersect, it may be possible that C is internal to D. This can be checked by algorithm *HPOINT* by testing some point of C if it is internal to D. C and $P(D)$ do not intersect if and only if both tests fail.

6.5.4. Curve-Area Intersection Computation

To actually compute the intersection of a curve with an area, we present the hierarchical algorithm *HCRVARA*. Given the arc trees of a curve C and a simple closed curve D, *HCRVARA* computes $C \cap P(D)$. The initiation and the loop of *HCRVARA* are identical to the corresponding sections of algorithm *HCRVCRV*. As *HCRVCRV*, *HCRVARA* proceeds until one of two conditions is met: (i) there are no more tagged edges, or (ii) the maximum resolution has been reached.

In case (i), it may be that C is internal to D. A point query on some point of C suffices to decide if that is the case. In case (ii), each tagged edge of C_{app} is intersected with each tagged edge of D_{app} and subdivided at the intersection points into disjoint edge segments. Now each edge segment of C_{app} is either internal or external to D_{app}. *HCRVARA* performs a point query for some point of C_{app} to see if it is internal or external. Starting from that point, *HCRVARA* performs a traversal of C_{app} to label each of its edges. The label is alternately internal or external, changing at each intersection point. Some special handling is required for edges of C_{app} that coincide with edges of D_{app}; see figure 6.19 for an example. For simplicity, this case is not considered further here.

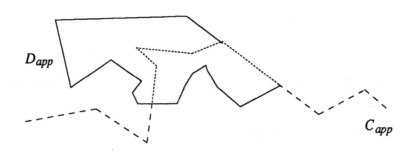

Figure 6.19: The dotted segments of C_{app} are internal, the broken segments external.

Finally, *HCRVARA* replaces all untagged internal edges of C_{app} by the corresponding edges of maximum resolution, and returns the internal edges and edge segments of C_{app}. It follows a more exact description of *HCRVARA*.

Algorithm HCRVARA

Input: The arc trees T_C and T_D of a curve C and a simple closed curve D.

Output: $C \cap P(D)$

(1) Set the approximation polygons C_{app} to C_0, D_{app} to D_0, and k to zero.

(2) For each pair of edges $e_{k,i}$ of C_{app} and $f_{k,j}$ of D_{app}, check if the two ellipses $E_{k,i}$ and $F_{k,j}$ intersect. If yes, tag $e_{k,i}$ and $f_{k,j}$.

(3) If there are no tagged edges, return *no intersection* and stop.

(4) Otherwise, if k is less than the maximum resolution, $\min(depth\,(T_C), depth\,(T_D))$, replace each tagged edge $e_{k,i}$ of C_{app} by the two edges $e_{k+1,2i-1}$ and $e_{k+1,2i}$. Similarly for each tagged edge $f_{k,j}$ of D_{app}. Increase k by one and repeat from (2).

(5) Otherwise, the maximum resolution has been reached. Intersect each tagged edge $e_{k,i}$ with each tagged edge $f_{k,j}$ and subdivide the edges $e_{k,i}$ at their intersection points into disjoint segments.

(6) Perform a point query for some point P of C_{app} to see if P is internal or external to D_{app}.

(7) Starting from P, traverse C_{app} and label its edges. The label is alternately internal or external, changing at each intersection point.

(8) Replace the internal untagged edges by the corresponding edges of maximum resolution.

(9) Return the internal edges and edge segments of C_{app}.

We implemented this algorithm on a VAX 8800 with the same modifications as in the case of *HCURVES*. Figures 6.20 and 6.21 give two examples for the output of the algorithm at various maximum resolutions r. The dotted curves are the final approximations D_{app}, respectively.

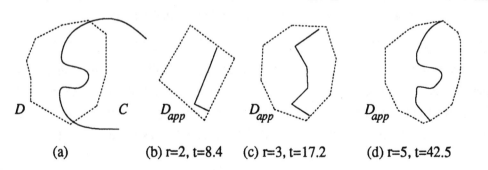

(a)   (b) r=2, t=8.4   (c) r=3, t=17.2   (d) r=5, t=42.5

Figure 6.20: C is a spline with 10 knots, D a spline with 18 knots.

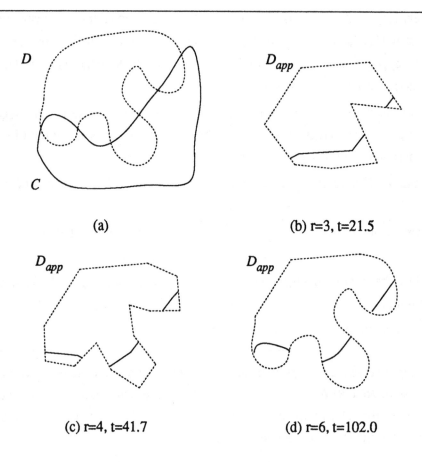

(a)

(b) r=3, t=21.5

(c) r=4, t=41.7

(d) r=6, t=102.0

Figure 6.21: Both C and D are splines with 20 knots.

Again, the running times do not increase quadratically with the number of edges, 2^r, or with the complexity of the input curves. In fact, the increase in CPU time is about cubical in r, i.e. polylogarithmic in the number of edges. Figure 6.22 shows the increase in CPU time for both figures and for resolutions $r=2$ through $r=7$.

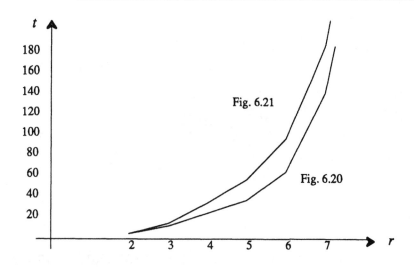

Figure 6.22: CPU time t of algorithm *HCRVARA* at various resolutions r.

6.5.5. Area-Area Intersection Detection

Given the arc trees of two closed curves C and D, it is now easy to detect if the enclosed point sets $P(C)$ and $P(D)$ intersect. First, one employs algorithm *HCURVES* to check C and D for intersection. If the two curves do not intersect, it may be possible that C is internal to D, or vice versa. This can be checked by algorithm *HPOINT* by testing some point of C if it is internal to D, and some point of D if it is internal to C. The two areas do not intersect if and only if all tests fail.

6.5.6. Area-Area Set Operations

Given the arc trees of two closed curve C and D, the intersection of $P(C)$ and $P(D)$ can now be computed as follows. First, one employs algorithm HCRVARA to compute $C \cap P(D)$ and $D \cap P(C)$. The resulting curves form the boundary of the intersection $P(C) \cap P(D)$. Some special handling is required for those edge segments that C and D have in common. HCRVARA has to be modified such that it marks these segments in its output. They are included in the boundary if and only if the corresponding edges of C and D have the same orientation; see figure 6.23.

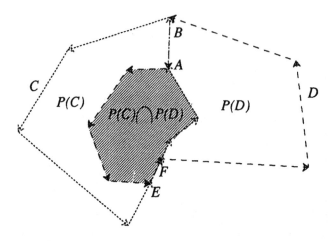

Figure 6.23: *EF* is included in the boundary of $P(C) \cap P(D)$, *AB* is not.

We implemented this algorithm on a VAX 8800 with the same modifications as in the case of *HCURVES*. Figures 6.24 and 6.25 give two examples for the performance of the algorithm at various maximum resolutions r. The broken curves are the final approximations C_{app} and D_{app}, respectively. Again, the running times do not increase quadratically with the maximum resolution or with the complexity of the input curves.

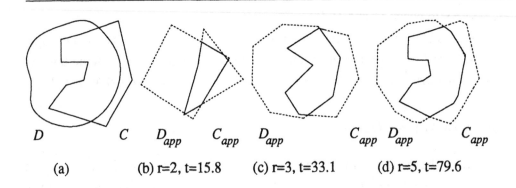

(a)	(b) r=2, t=15.8	(c) r=3, t=33.1	(d) r=5, t=79.6

Figure 6.24: C is a spline with 10 knots, D a spline with 20 knots.

To obtain the boundary of the union $P(C) \cup P(D)$, one computes those segments of C that are external to D and those segments of D that are external to C.

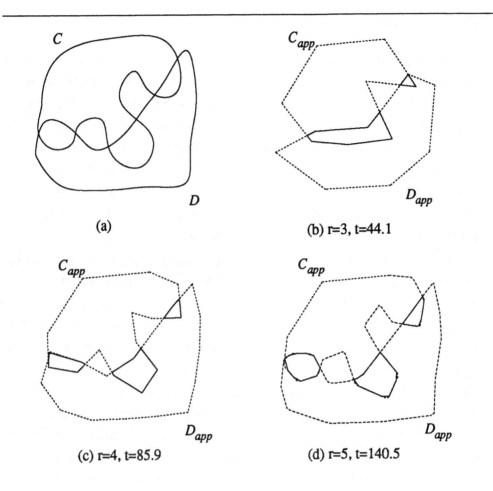

Figure 6.25: Both C and D are splines with 20 knots.

Again, the edge segments that C and D have in common are included if and only if the corresponding edges of C and D have the same orientation.

To retrieve the boundary of the difference $P(C)-P(D)$, one computes those segments of C that are external to D and those segments of D that are internal to C. The edge segments that C and D have in common are included if and only if the corresponding edges of C and D do *not* have the same orientation.

6.6. Implementation in a Database System

As the previous sections have shown, the arc tree is an efficient scheme to represent curves. In large-scale geometric applications such as geography or robotics, is is usually most efficient to have a separate data management component and to maintain a geometric database to store a large number of geometric objects. In order to use the arc tree representation scheme efficiently in this context, it is therefore necessary to embed arc trees as complex objects in the database system. This section will discuss several ways to perform this embedding; we will restrict our analysis to relational databases. For a more extensive analysis of geometric modeling in database systems, see [Meie86] or [Kemp87a].

There are three major ways to implement complex objects in an extensible relational database system such as POSTGRES [Ston86a], DASDBS [Paul87], or XRS [Meie87]. First, one may organize the data of a complex object in relational form and represent the object as a set of tuples, each marked with a unique object identifier. Then the algorithms may be either programmed in an external host language with embedded query language commands [RTI84], or within the database system by means of user-defined data types and operators [Wong85, Kemp87b]. These approaches have been used in earlier attempts to extend relational database systems to applications in geography and robotics [Kung84, Gunt87c]. Second, one supports a procedural data type to store expressions in the query language or any other programming language directly in the database. This approach is emphasized in the POSTGRES database system [Ston86c]. Third, one may define an abstract data type (ADT) with corresponding operators and abstract indices; see for example [Ston83]. The importance and suitability of ADT mechanisms for geometric data management has also been discussed by Schek [Sche86]. The following sections will discuss these approaches in turn and evaluate their suitability to embed arc trees in a relational database.

6.6.1. The Pure Relational Approach

The traditional approach would be to represent a complex object as a set of tuples, i.e. as a relation or subrelation. For the representation of an arc tree, the following relation may be used.

arctreenodes (tree-id = int, node-id = int, point-x = real, point-y = real,
    left-son = int, right-son = int)

Then the algorithms for intersection detection and so on are coded in a general-purpose programming language (the *host language*) that allows the embedding of query commands to access the database. In the case of INGRES [Ston76], one may use, for example, EQUEL/FORTRAN [RTI84].

For this approach, the relational data model as defined by Codd [Codd70] would be sufficient. It would not be necessary to extend the data model by new concepts such as special data types, and query optimization could be carried out as usual. Nevertheless, we do not believe that this approach will be very efficient. For each access to a tree node it is necessary to activate the interface between host language and the database system. In order to get the *left–son* node of a given node N, for example, it is necessary to process the following query.

range of a1, a2 is arctreenodes
retrieve (a1.all)
where a1.node-id = a2.left-son
and a2.node-id = N

This query involves a join of the relation *arctreenodes* with itself. Then the resulting tuple has to be returned to the host language before the execution of the program can continue. This is a major effort to retrieve just one node, which may slow down the overall performance of our algorithms considerably.

6.6.2. User Defined Data Types and Operators

A variation of this approach would be to represent the arc tree as above, but to program the algorithms *within* the query language by means of user defined data types and operators [Wong85, Kemp87b].

Here, the user has to define the geometric data types and operators that are needed in this context, based on the data types and operators provided by the database system. For example, one may define a data type *line* in two dimensions as

define type line (phase = real, dist = real)

where *phase* denotes the angle between the line and the x-axis, and *dist* is the distance between the line and the origin. Then one defines an operator *intersect* as

define operator intersect (l1=line, l2=line) as z = boolean
where z=1 if l1.phase ≠ l2.phase or l1.dist = l2.dist

Eventually, one will be able to program arc tree algorithms within the extended query language. Clearly, each query Q that uses any of the user defined data types and operators can be mapped onto a query $\bar{Q}$ in the basic query language. Then the query optimization can be performed on $\bar{Q}$ in the usual manner. Moreover, there will be opportunities to perform some kind of global query optimization [Sell85] because the queries occuring during an arc tree operation do not have to be processed one by one, as in the case of the host language approach.

One problem with this approach is that it requires the definition of a lot of data types and operators before algorithms can be coded. Even more important, it is quite doubtful if the database can provide an efficient runtime environment for the program execution. Any query Q has to be translated during runtime into a query $\bar{Q}$ in the basic query language. $\bar{Q}$ may be quite complex, especially if the user-defined data types and operators are deeply nested. Nevertheless, this approach seems somewhat promising and should be included in a practical performance analysis.

6.6.3. Procedure as a Data Type

Another method to support complex objects is to introduce a procedural data type; in particular, a data type *query* seems to be useful. This approach has first been suggested by Stonebraker [Ston84] and it is currently being implemented in POSTGRES. The procedural data type refers to complex components by means of a retrieval command. This approach provides easy access to lower level components and efficient support for shared subobjects, for complex objects with many levels of subobjects, and for complex objects with unpredictable composition [Ston86c].

Consider the following POSTGRES relation *object* with two tuples *apple* and *orange* and three underlying relations *polygon*, *circle*, and *line*.

name	desc
apple	*retrieve (polygon.all) where polygon.id = 10* *retrieve (circle.all) where circle.id = 40*
orange	*retrieve (line.all) where line.id = 17* *retrieve (polygon.all) where polygon.id = 10*

Clearly, the polygon 10 is a complex object that is shared by both *apple* and *orange*. To retrieve the area of the shared polygon, for example, one may use the multiple-dot notation [Zani83] as follows.

retrieve (object.desc.polygon.area) where object.name = 'apple'

In order to improve performance, it is usually useful to precompute access plans or even answers to stored queries. This precomputation step makes the query optimization somewhat more complicated, but it improves overall efficiency. As discussed in [Ston86c], the procedural data type also provides efficient support for complex objects with many levels of subobjects and complex objects with unpredictable composition.

The arc tree is certainly an object with many levels of subobjects, but it has a very regular structure and no shared subobjects. Furthermore, the set of operators to be performed is very limited, and any selective access to lower level subtrees is embedded in a more complex operator, such as union or intersection, that starts out at the root of the tree and works its way down from there. We therefore do not believe that the procedural data type is an adequate embedding for arc trees; it is too complicated because it is too powerful. We advocate to use the simpler ADT scheme as described in the following section.

6.6.4. Abstract Data Types

Although the arc tree is a useful representation scheme for the most important geometric operators, it should not necessarily be visible to the user. On the contrary, all set and search operators should be executed *without* revealing the internal representation scheme - the arc tree - to the user. The only operator where the internal representation may be visible to the user is the rendering of approximations of the curve. But even then, it seems preferable to offer an operator that maps an abstract object of type *curve* and a resolution into an approximation of the curve. Note that for none of the common operators the user needs to have explicit access to subtrees or to retrieve or manipulate details of the arc tree. On the other hand, it is important to implement the algorithms for set and search operations as efficiently as possible. The algorithms are complex, and their performance should not be impeded unnecessarily by an insufficient runtime environment or an inadequate implementation language.

Because of these considerations we believe that an embedding of the arc tree as an abstract data type (ADT) into an extensible database system is the superior solution to the problem. An ADT is an encapsulation of a data structure (so that its implementation details are not visible to an outside client procedure) along with a collection of related operators on this encapsulated structure. The canonical example of an ADT is a stack with related operators *new*, *push*, *pop* and *empty*.

In our case, the user is given an ADT *curve*; each curve is represented internally as an arc tree, but this fact is completely transparent to the user. The operators defined on curves are given in the following table.

operator	operand-1	operand-2	result
approximation	curve	integer	curve
point inclusion test	curve	point	boolean
curve-curve intersection detection	curve	curve	boolean
curve-curve intersection computation	curve	curve	set of points
curve-area intersection detection	curve	(closed) curve	boolean
curve-area intersection computation	curve	(closed) curve	set of curves
area-area intersection detection	(closed) curve	(closed) curve	boolean
area-area intersection computation	(closed) curve	(closed) curve	set of (closed) curves
area-area union computation	(closed) curve	(closed) curve	set of (closed) curves
area-area difference computation	(closed) curve	(closed) curve	set of (closed) curves

Internally, all of these operators can be implemented in a high level programming language such as LISP or C++. Because the nodes of the arc trees are accessed along the child pointers of the tree, it will be useful to store nodes near their ancestor nodes. Note that it is not necessary to define a separate data type for *closed* curves. Each operator that requires the input curves to be closed may just extend its type checking by a test for closedness. Operators that return sets may just be implemented as relation-valued operators (such as the common *retrieve* command that may return relations as well as single tuples).

6.7. Summary

We presented the arc tree, a balanced binary tree that serves as an approximation scheme for curves. It is shown how the arc tree can be used to represent curves for efficient support of common set and search operators. The arc tree can be viewed as just one instance of a large class of approximation schemes that implement some hierarchy of detail. We gave an overview of several other approximation schemes that are based on the same idea, and indicated how to modify the arc tree algorithms to work with these schemes.

Several examples are given for the performance of our algorithms to compute set and search operators such as point inclusion or area-area intersection detection and computation. The results of the practical analysis are encouraging: in most cases, the computation of boolean operators such as point inclusion or intersection detection can be completed on the first four or five levels of the tree. Also, the computation of non-boolean operators such as intersection computation gives fairly good results even if one restricts the computation to the first few levels. Finally, it is described how to embed arc trees as complex objects in an extensible database system. It is argued that the embedding as an abstract data type is most efficient.

It is subject of future research to conduct a more comprehensive and systematic study of the arc tree algorithms and of the different possibilities to handle arc trees in an extensible database system. Also, we are planning to compare the arc tree to Ballard's strip tree and to Bezier curves, both theoretically and practically.

Chapter 7

Conclusions

The main theme of this book is the significance of suitable representation schemes for efficient geometric data management. While issues of representation are important in any kind of computing environment, they gain a particular weight when dealing with geometric data. There is a wide variety of geometric operators that are commonly used, and there is simply no single representation that provides efficient support for all of them. Compared to numeric operators, most geometric operators are hard to compute, and in order to be reasonably fast, one has to precompute and store intermediate results. A representation scheme can be viewed as the result of a precomputation: it is an intermediate result, which can be used for the computation of certain operators.

In this book, we first gave a survey of common representation schemes for geometric data. Following that, several new schemes were proposed and analyzed to determine which schemes are good for which operators.

In chapter 2 we described a general taxonomy for operators and representation schemes and gave a survey of common representation schemes for two- and three-dimensional geometric data. We pointed out the significance of uniqueness, distance functions, and of invariant parts in a representation scheme. All of these features are especially important for the efficient support of recognition operators. Many representation schemes can be normalized to be unique and to have invariances with respect to similarity operators. Also, we discussed how to define distance functions that measure the difference between two geometric objects. As an example, we described how to use Fourier descriptors to implement normalization and distance functions.

Chapter 3 introduced polyhedral chains as a new representation scheme for polyhedral data in arbitrary dimensions. Each polyhedral point set is represented as an algebraic sum of simple polyhedra. In particular, we considered *convex* polyhedral chains and discussed an implementation, where each convex cell is represented as an intersection of halfspaces and encoded in a ternary vector. The notion of vertices or adjacencies is abandoned completely. We showed how it is then possible to decompose the computation of set operators on polyhedral point sets into two steps. The first step consists of a collection of vector operations; the second step is a garbage collection where vectors that represent empty cells are eliminated. All results of the garbage collection can be cached in the vectors in such a way that the garbage collector never has to do any computation more than once. As the database is learning more and more information through the garbage collector, it will be able to detect empty cells immediately such that no additional test for emptiness is required. As a result, the computation of set operators becomes faster as the system is used. No special treatment of singular intersection cases is required. This approach to set operations is significantly different from algorithms that have been proposed in the past.

In order to carry out the garbage collection efficiently, an algorithm is needed that detects quickly if two given convex cells intersect. In chapter 4 we digressed into theoretical computational geometry and presented a dual approach to detect intersections of hyperplanes and convex polyhedra in arbitrary dimensions. In d dimensions, the time complexities of the dual algorithms are $O(2^d \log n)$ for the hyperplane-polyhedron intersection problem, and $O((2d)^{d-1}\log^{d-1} n)$ for the polyhedron-polyhedron intersection problem. In two dimensions, these time bounds are achieved with linear space and preprocessing. In three dimensions, the hyperplane-polyhedron intersection problem is also solved with linear space and preprocessing, which is an improvement over previously known results. Quadratic space and preprocessing, however, is required for the polyhedron-polyhedron intersection problem. For general d, the dual algorithms require $O(n^{2^d})$ space and preprocessing. These results are the first of their kind for dimensions larger than three, and the first that readily extend to unbounded polyhedra.

In chapter 5 we discussed geometric index structures, which are representation schemes to support search operators such as point and range searches. We presented the design of a database index for multidimensional geometric data, termed cell tree. All data objects in the database are represented as convex chains. The cell tree indexes the set of cells by means of a binary space partitioning. It is a fully dynamic data structure, i.e. insertions and deletions may be interleaved with searches and no periodic reorganization is required. Moreover, the cell tree is designed for paged memory; it represents an attempt to minimize the number of page faults per search operation.

In chapter 6 we presented the arc tree, another hierarchical data structure, which serves as an approximation scheme to represent arbitrary curves. The arc tree represents a curve of length l by a balanced binary tree such that any subtree whose root is on the k-th tree level is representing a subcurve of length $l/2^k$. Each tree level is associated with an approximation of the curve; lower levels correspond to approximations of higher resolution. Based on this data structure, we described and analyzed hierarchical algorithms for several set and search operators. These algorithms start out near the root of the tree and try to solve the queries at a very coarse resolution. If that is not possible, the resolution is increased where necessary. The results of the practical analysis are encouraging: in most cases, the computation of boolean operators such as point inclusion test or intersection detection can be completed on the first four or five levels of the tree. Also, the computation of non-boolean operators such as intersection computation gives fairly good results even if one restricts the computation to the first few levels. The arc tree can be viewed as just one instance of a large class of approximation schemes that implement some hierarchy of detail. We gave an overview of several other approximation schemes that are based on this idea, and indicated how to modify the arc tree algorithms to work with these schemes. Several possibilities were described to embed arc trees into an extensible database system such as POSTGRES, and it seems that the embedding as an abstract data type is most promising.

As it should be clear from the above, in geometric computing it is necessary to compute and store multiple representations of the given data in order to have the most efficient representation available for every operator. In numeric computing, on the other hand, one representation is usually sufficient. The maintenance of multiple representations brings about difficult problems concerning their availability and mutual consistency.

Multiple representations are very efficiently supported by two database mechanisms, namely views and indices. To use views, some representation is declared the main representation and stored explicitly; other representations are views of this main representation. In order to make the various representations more available, these views should be precomputed and stored as well. In many cases, view updates may be admissible, as they can be translated into updates of the main representation. The consistency of the representations is monitored by demons that invalidate a precomputed view if necessary (i.e. if the corresponding main representation changes).

Another way to implement multiple representations are database indices, such as the B-tree, the R-tree or the cell tree. The construction of an index may require a lot of computation, but once it is constructed, it represents the underlying data in such a way that search operators can be computed on this representation very efficiently. Of course, any update to the data may cause the index representation to change as well, which brings up the need for efficient index update algorithms.

Given the fact, that views and indices are standard features in database systems, it seems preferable to have geometric data management performed by an off-the-shelf database system, rather than by a user-written software module. Extensible database systems such as POSTGRES [Ston86a], DASDBS [Paul87], or XRS [Meie87] also provide facilities to manage complex geometric data objects, to define indices, and to support powerful artificial intelligence techniques such as rules. Furthermore, a database system has other useful features, such as a well-defined data model, concurrency control, recovery mechanisms, or normalization techniques to avoid redundancies. Also, database systems are known for their ability to scale up well to manage larger amounts of data. This is often not the case with user-written data managers, which may cause problems if the given application expands more than anticipated.

For the near future, we are planning to apply our results and related work in a practical setting. We intend to use POSTGRES to perform the geometric data management of a major robotics and vision application. This project should give us some insight into the practical problems with various geometric representation schemes that we proposed. We are planning to compare the various possibilities to embed representation schemes as complex objects in POSTGRES. Furthermore, the POSTGRES implementation will show how mature the new generation of relational database systems really is, and how their performance compares with special-purpose data managers.

References

[Ayal85]   Ayala, D., P. Brunet, R. Juan, and I. Navazo, Object representation by means of nonminimal division quadtrees and octrees, *ACM Trans. on Graphics* **4**, 1 (January 1985), pages 41-59.

[Ball81]   Ballard, D. H., Strip trees: A hierarchical representation for curves, *Comm. of the ACM* **24**, 5 (May 1981), pages 310-321.

[Baye72]   Bayer, R. and E. M. McCreight, Organization and maintenance of large ordered indices, *Acta Informatica* **1**, 3 (1972), pages 1-21.

[Bent80]   Bentley, J. L. and J. B. Saxe, Decomposable searching problems #1: Static to dynamic transformation, *J. of Algorithms* **1** (1980), pages 301-358.

[Besl85]   Besl, P. J. and R. C. Jain, Three-dimensional object recognition, *Computing Surveys* **17**, 1 (March 1985).

[Bezi74]   Bezier, P. E., Mathematical and practical possibilities of UNISURF, in *Computer Aided Geometric Design*, Academic Press, New York, NY, 1974, pages 127-152.

[Blum67]   Blum, H., A transformation for extracting new descriptors of shape, in *Models for the perception of speech and visual form*, W. Wathen-Dunn (ed.), MIT Press, Cambridge, Ma., 1967.

[Bohm84]   Bohm, W., Efficient evaluation of splines, *Computing* **33** (1984), pages 171-177.

[Brow79]   Brown, K. Q., *Geometric transformations for fast geometric algorithms*, Ph.D. dissertation, Carnegie-Mellon University, Pittsburgh, Pa., Dec. 1979.

[Brun87]   Brunet, P. and D. Ayala, Extended octree representation of free form surfaces, *Computer-Aided Geometric Design* **4** (1987), pages 141-154.

[Burt77]   Burton, W., Representation of many-sided polygons and polygonal lines for rapid processing, *Comm. of the ACM* **20**, 3 (March 1977), pages 166-171.

[Carl87]   Carlbom, I., An algorithm for geometric set operations using cellular subdivision techniques, *IEEE Comp. Graphics App.*, May 1987, pages 44-55.

[Chaz80]   Chazelle, B. and D. P. Dobkin, Detection is easier than computation, in *Proc. 12th Annual ACM Symposium on Theory of Computing*, 1980, pages 146-153.

[Chaz84]   Chazelle, B., Convex partitions of polyhedra: A lower bound and worst-case optimal algorithm, *SIAM J. Comput.* **13**, 3 (1984), pages 488-507.

[Chaz87]   Chazelle, B. and D. P. Dobkin, Intersection of convex objects in two and three dimensions, *J. ACM* **34**, 1 (Jan. 1987), pages 1-27.

[Clar87]   Clarkson, K. L., New applications of random sampling in computational geometry, *Discrete Comput. Geometry* **2** (1987), pages 195-222.

[Codd70]   Codd, E., A relational model of data for large shared data bases, *Comm. of the ACM* **13**, 6 (June 1970), pages 377-387.

[Come79]   Comer, D., The ubiquitous B-tree, *Computing Surveys* **11**, 2 (1979), pages 121-138.

[Dant63]   Dantzig, G. B., *Linear programming and its extensions*, Princeton University Press, Princeton, NJ, 1963.

[Debo78]   Deboor, C., *A practical guide to splines*, Springer-Verlag, Heidelberg, 1978.

[Dobk76]   Dobkin, D. P. and R. J. Lipton, Multidimensional searching problems, *SIAM J. Comput.* **5**, 2 (June 1976), pages 181-186.

[Dobk80]   Dobkin, D. P. and J. I. Munro, Efficient uses of the past, in *Proc. 21st Annual Symposium on Foundations of Computer Science*, Syracuse, NY, 1980, pages 200-206.

[Dobk83]   Dobkin, D. P. and D. G. Kirkpatrick, Fast detection of polyhedral intersection, *Theoret. Comput. Sci.* **27** (1983), pages 241-253.

[Dyer79]   Dyer, C. R. and A. Rosenfeld, Thinning algorithms for grayscale pictures, *IEEE Trans. Pattern Anal. Machine Intell.* **PAMI-1**, 1 (1979), pages 88-89.

[Edel86a] Edelsbrunner, H., L. J. Guibas, and J. Stolfi, Optimal point location in a monotone subdivision, *SIAM J. Comput.* **15**, 2 (1986), pages 317-340.

[Edel86b] Edelsbrunner, H., J. O'Rourke, and R. Seidel, Constructing arrangements of lines and hyperplanes with applications, *SIAM J. Comput.* **15**, 2 (1986), pages 341-363.

[Edel87] Edelsbrunner, H., *Algorithms in combinatorial geometry*, Springer-Verlag, Berlin, 1987.

[Falo87] Faloutsos, C., T. Sellis, and N. Roussopoulos, Analysis of object oriented spatial access methods, in *Proc. of ACM SIGMOD Conference on Management of Data*, San Francisco, Ca., June 1987.

[Faux79] Faux, I. D. and M. J. Pratt, *Computational geometry for design and manufacture*, Ellis Horwood, Chichester, Great Britain, 1979.

[Fink74] Finkel, R. A. and J. L. Bentley, Quad trees - A data structure for retrieval on composite keys, *Acta Informatica* **4** (1974), pages 1-9.

[Fran82] Franklin, W. R., Efficient polyhedron intersection and union, *Graphics Interface 82*, May 1982, pages 73-80.

[Fuch80] Fuchs, H., Z. Kedem, and B. Naylor, On visible surface generation by a priori tree structures, *Computer Graphics* **14**, 3 (June 1980).

[Fuch83] Fuchs, H., G. D. Abram, and E. D. Grant, Near real-time shaded display of rigid objects, *Computer Graphics* **17**, 3 (Summer 1983), pages 65-72.

[Gonz87] Gonzalez, R. C. and P. Wintz, *Digital image processing*, Addison-Wesley, Reading, Ma., 1987.

[Gree88] Greene, D., *An implementation and performance analysis of spatial data access methods*, U.C. Berkeley, Master's Report, Feb. 1988.

[Gunt87a] Gunther, O. and E. Wong, A dual space representation for geometric data, in *Proc. 13th International Conference on Very Large Data Bases*, Brighton, England, Sept. 1987.

[Gunt87b] Gunther, O. and E. Wong, A dual approach to detect polyhedral intersections in arbitrary dimensions, in *Proc. 25th Annual Allerton Conf. on Comm., Control and Comp.*, Oct. 1987.

[Gunt87c] Gunther, O., An expert database system for the overland search problem, in *Proc. BTW' 87 - Database Systems for Office Automation, Engineering, and Scientific Applications*, Informatik-Fachberichte No. 136, Springer, Berlin, 1987.

[Gunt88] Gunther, O. and J. Bilmes, *A performance analysis of the cell tree and other spatial access methods*, in preparation, 1988.

[Gutt84] Guttman, A., R-trees: A dynamic index structure for spatial searching, in *Proc. of ACM SIGMOD Conference on Management of Data*, Boston, Ma., June 1984.

[Hinr85] Hinrichs, K. H., *The grid file system: Implementation and case studies of applications*, ETH Zürich, Dissertation No. 7734, 1985.

[Hopc87] Hopcroft, J. E. and D. B. Krafft, The challenge of robotics for computer science, in *Algorithmic and geometric aspects of robotics*, Advances in robotics, Vol. 1, C. Yap and J. Schwartz (eds.), Lawrence Erlbaum Associates, Hillsdale, NJ, 1987.

[Imai86] Imai, H. and M. Iri, Computational-geometric methods for polygonal approximations of a curve, *Comp. Vision Graph. Image Proc.* **36** (1986), pages 31-41.

[Kemp87a] Kemper, A. and M. Wallrath, An analysis of geometric modeling in database systems, *Computing Surveys* **19**, 1 (March 1987), pages 47-91.

[Kemp87b] Kemper, A., P. C. Lockemann, and M. Wallrath, An object-oriented database system for engineering applications, in *Proc. of ACM SIGMOD Conference on Management of Data*, San Francisco, Ca., May 1987.

[Krie86] Kriegel, H. P. and B. Seeger, Multidimensional order preserving linear hashing with partial expansions, in *Proc. International Conference on Database Theory*, Lecture Notes in Computer Science, Springer, Berlin, 1986.

[Kung79] Kung, H. T., Systolic arrays, *Computer* **11**, 4 (Dec. 1979), pages 397-409.

[Kung84] Kung, R., E. Hanson, Y. Ioannidis, T. Sellis, L. Shapiro, and M. Stonebraker, Heuristic search in data base systems, in *Proc. 1st International Conference on Expert Database Systems*, Kiowah, S.C., Oct. 1984.

[Lee84]   Lee, D. T. and F. P. Preparata, Computational geometry - a survey, *IEEE Trans. on Computers* **C-33**, 12 (Dec. 1984), pages 1072-1101.

[Mand77]   Mandelbrot, B. B., *Fractals: Form, Chance and Dimension*, W. H. Freeman & Co., San Francisco, Ca., 1977.

[Mant82]   Mantyla, M. and R. Sulonen, GWB: A solid modeler with Euler operators, *IEEE Comp. Graphics App.*, Sept. 1982, pages 17-31.

[Mant83]   Mantyla, M. and M. Tamminen, Localized set operations for solid modeling, *Computer Graphics*, July 1983, pages 279-288.

[Megi84]   Megiddo, N., Linear programming in linear time when the dimension is fixed, *J. ACM* **31**, 1 (Jan. 1984), pages 114-127.

[Meie86]   Meier, A., Applying relational database techniques to solid modeling, *Computer-Aided Design* **18**, 6 (July/Aug. 1986).

[Meie87]   Meier, A., *Erweiterung relationaler Datenbanksysteme für technische Anwendungen*, Informatik-Fachberichte No. 135, Springer, Berlin, 1987.

[Meis88]   Meiser, S., Point location in arrangements, in *Proc. of the 4th Workshop on Computational Geometry*, Lecture Notes in Computer Science, Springer, Berlin, 1988.

[Nava86]   Navazo, I., J. Fontdecaba, and P. Brunet, Extended octrees, between CSG trees and boundary representations, in *Proc. of the EUROGRAPHICS'87 Conference*, North-Holland, Amsterdam, April 1986.

[Nayl86]   Naylor, B. F. and W. C. Thibault, *Application of BSP trees to raytracing and CSG evaluation*, Georgia Institute of Technology, Technical Report GIT-ICS 86/03, Feb. 1986.

[Newe80]   Newell, M. E. and C. H. Sequin, The inside story on self-intersecting polygons, *LAMBDA*, Second Quarter 1980.

[Newm79]   Newman, W. M. and R. F. Sproull, *Principles of interactive computer graphics*, McGraw-Hill, New York, NY, 1979.

[Niev82]   Nievergelt, J. and F. P. Preparata, Plane-sweep algorithms for intersecting geometric figures, *Comm. of the ACM* **25**, 10 (Oct. 1982), pages 739-747.

[Niev84] Nievergelt, J., H. Hinterberger, and K. C. Sevcik, The grid file: An adaptable, symmetric multikey file structure, *ACM Trans. on Database Systems* **9**, 1 (March 1984), pages 38-71.

[Paul87] Paul, H.-B., H.-J. Schek, M. H. Scholl, G. Weikum, and U. Deppisch, Architecture and implementation of the Darmstadt database kernel system (DASDBS), in *Proc. of ACM SIGMOD Conference on Management of Data*, San Francisco, Ca., May 1987.

[Pavl82] Pavlidis, T., *Algorithms for graphics and image processing*, Computer Science Press, Rockville, Md., 1982.

[Pers77] Persoon, E. and K. S. Fu, Shape discrimination using Fourier descriptors, *IEEE Trans. Syst. Man Cybern.* **7**, 3 (March 1977), pages 170-179.

[Ponc87] Ponce, J. and O. Faugeras, An object centered hierarchical representation for 3D objects: the prism tree, *Comp. Vision Graph. Image Proc.* **38** (1987), pages 1-28.

[Prep79] Preparata, F. P. and D. E. Muller, Finding the intersection of a set of N half-spaces in time $O(N \log N)$, *Theoret. Comput. Sci.* **8** (1979), pages 45-55.

[Prep85] Preparata, F. P. and M. I. Shamos, *Computational geometry*, Springer-Verlag, New York, NY, 1985.

[Putn86] Putnam, L. K. and P. A. Subrahmanyam, Boolean operations on n-dimensional objects, *IEEE Comp. Graphics App.* **6**, 6 (June 1986).

[RTI84] RTI, Relational Technology Inc., *INGRES/EQUEL/FORTRAN User's guide, version 3.0, VAX/VMS*, Oct. 1984.

[Requ80] Requicha, A. A. G., Representations for rigid solids: theory, methods, and systems, *Computing Surveys* **12**, 4 (Dec. 1980).

[Requ82] Requicha, A. A. G. and H. B. Voelcker, Solid modeling: a historical summary and contemporary assessment, *IEEE Comp. Graphics App.*, March 1982, pages 9-24.

[Requ83] Requicha, A. A. G. and H. B. Voelcker, Solid modeling: current status and research directions, *IEEE Comp. Graphics App.*, Oct. 1983, pages 25-37.

[Requ85]   Requicha, A. A. G. and H. B. Voelcker, Boolean operations in solid modeling: Boundary evaluation and merging algorithms, in *Proc. IEEE*, Jan. 1985, pages 30-44.

[Robi81]   Robinson, J. T., The k-d-b tree: A search structure for large multidimensional dynamic indexes, in *Proc. of ACM SIGMOD Conference on Management of Data*, April 1981.

[Rock70]   Rockafellar, R. T., *Convex Analysis,* Princeton University Press, Princeton, NJ, 1970.

[Rous85]   Roussopoulos, N. and D. Leifker, Direct spatial search on pictorial databases using packed R-trees, in *Proc. of ACM SIGMOD Conference on Management of Data*, Austin, Tx., June 1985.

[Sala84]   Salari, E. and P. Siy, The ridge-seeking method for obtaining the skeleton of digital images, *IEEE Trans. Syst. Man Cyb.* **SMC-14**, 3 (1984), pages 524-528.

[Same84]   Samet, H., The quadtree and related hierarchical data structures, *Computing Surveys* **16**, 2 (June 1984), pages 187-260.

[Same85]   Samet, H. and R. E. Webber, Storing a collection of polygons using quadtrees, *ACM Trans. on Graphics* **4**, 3 (July 1985), pages 182-222.

[Sche86]   Schek, H.-J., Datenbanksysteme für die Verwaltung geometrischer Objekte, in *Proc. of the 16th GI Annual Meeting*, Informatik-Fachberichte No. 126, Springer, Berlin, Oct. 1986.

[Sell85]   Sellis, T., Global query optimization, in *Proc. of ACM SIGMOD Conference on Management of Data*, Austin, Tx., May 1985.

[Sell87]   Sellis, T., N. Roussopoulos, and C. Faloutsos, The R+-tree: A dynamic index for multi-dimensional objects, in *Proc. 13th International Conference on Very Large Data Bases*, Brighton, England, Sept. 1987.

[Sequ83]   Sequin, C. H., M. Segal, and P. Wensley, *UNIGRAFIX 2.0 User's manual and tutorial*, U.C. Berkeley, Technical Report No. UCB/CSD 83/161, Dec. 1983.

[Sequ85]   Sequin, C. H. and P. R. Wensley, Visible feature return at object resolution, *IEEE Comp. Graphics App.* **5**, 6 (May 1985).

[Six86]   Six, H.-W. and P. Widmayer, Hintergrundspeicherstrukturen für aus-
            gedehnte Objekte, in *Tagungsband GI - 16. Jahrestagung*, Informatik-
            Fachberichte No. 126, Springer, Berlin, Oct. 1986.

[Ston76]   Stonebraker, M., E. Wong, P. Kreps, and G. Held, The design and
            implementation of INGRES, *ACM Trans. on Database Systems* **1**, 3
            (Sept. 1976), pages 189-222.

[Ston83]   Stonebraker, M., B. Rubenstein, and A. Guttman, Application of
            abstract data types and abstract indices to CAD data, in *Proc. Engineer-
            ing Applications Stream of ACM SIGMOD Conference*, San Jose, Ca.,
            May 1983.

[Ston84]   Stonebraker, M., E. Anderson, E. Hanson, and B. Rubenstein, QUEL as
            a data type, in *Proc. of ACM SIGMOD Conference on Management of
            Data*, Boston, Ma., June 1984.

[Ston86a]   Stonebraker, M. and L. Rowe, The design of POSTGRES, in *Proc. of
            ACM SIGMOD Conference on Management of Data*, Washington, DC,
            June 1986.

[Ston86b]   Stonebraker, M., T. Sellis, and E. Hanson, An analysis of rule indexing
            implementations in data base systems, in *Proc. of the 1st International
            Conference on Expert Data Base Systems*, April 1986.

[Ston86c]   Stonebraker, M., Object management in POSTGRES using procedures,
            in *Proc. 1986 International Workshop on Object-Oriented Database
            Systems*, Asilomar, Ca., Sept. 1986.

[Tamm82]   Tamminen, M., Efficient spatial access to a database, in *Proc. of ACM
            SIGMOD Conference on Management of Data*, May 1982.

[Tilo80]   Tilove, R. B., Set membership classification: A unified approach to
            geometric intersection problems, *IEEE Trans. on Computers* **C-29**, 10
            (Oct. 1980), pages 874-883.

[Tilo84a]   Tilove, R. B., A null object algorithm for constructive solid geometry,
            Comm. of the ACM **27**, 7 (July 1984).

[Tilo84b]   Tilove, R. B., A. A. G. Requicha, and M. R. Hopkins, Efficient editing
            of solid models by exploiting structural and spatial locality, *Computer-
            Aided Geometric Design* **1** (1984), pages 227-239.

[Whit57]   Whitney, H., *Geometric integration theory*, Princeton University Press, Princeton, NJ, 1957.

[Will82]   Willard, D. E., Polygon retrieval, *SIAM J. Comput.* **11**, 1 (Feb. 1982), pages 149-165.

[Wong85]   Wong, E., *Extended domain types and specification of user defined operators*, U.C. Berkeley, Memorandum No. UCB/ERL/M85/3, Feb. 1985.

[Zahn72]   Zahn, C. T. and R. Z. Roskies, Fourier descriptors for plane closed curves, *IEEE Trans. on Computers* **C-21**, 3 (1972), pages 269-281.

[Zani83]   Zaniolo, C., The database language GEM, in *Proc. of ACM SIGMOD Conference on Management of Data*, San Jose, Ca., May 1983.

[Zhan84]   Zhang, T. Y. and C. Y. Suen, A fast parallel algorithm for thinning digital patterns, *Comm. of the ACM* **27**, 3 (March 1984), pages 236-239.